D1526283

A Rock in a Weary Land

My God is a rock in a weary land,
My God is a rock in a weary land,
Shelter in a time of storm.

—Spiritual

A Rock in a Weary Land

The African Methodist Episcopal Church
During the Civil War and Reconstruction

CLARENCE E. WALKER

Louisiana State University Press
Baton Rouge and London

Copyright © 1982 by Louisiana State University Press
All rights reserved
Manufactured in the United States of America

Designer: Joanna Hill
Typeface: Sabon
Typesetter: G & S Typesetters, Inc.
Printing and binding: Thomson-Shore, Inc.

LIBRARY OF CONGRESS CATALOGING IN PUBLICATION DATA

Walker, Clarence Earl.
    A rock in a weary land.

    Revision of thesis (Ph.D.)—University of California, Berkeley, 1976.
    Bibliography: p.
    Includes index.
    1. African Methodist Episcopal Church—History.   I. Title.
BX8443.W27   1981   287'.83   81-11731
ISBN 0-8071-0883-9   AACR2

287. 81X
W151

82041235

IN MEMORY OF
Clarence Walker, Julia Craft Walker,
and Della Mae Franklin Walker

Contents

Acknowledgments

In the course of researching and writing this book I have incurred a number of debts. I would like to thank the Institute of Race and Community Relations of the University of California at Berkeley, the Ford Foundation, and the Wesleyan University Faculty Research Fund for financial support. Professors Robert Abzug, Lucille Birnbaum, Robert Blauner, Douglas Daniels, Nathan Huggins, Lawrence W. Levine, Kerby Miller, Winthrop Jordan, Kenneth Stampp, and Ronald Walters have read and criticized the manuscript at various stages of its preparation; the study has benefited greatly from their comments. A special word of thanks is extended to Professor Edmund L. Drago of the College of Charleston who shared ideas and materials with me while working on a book which parallels this one.

An equal debt of gratitude is expressed here to my Wesleyan colleagues, Professors Richard Buel, Samuel Cohn, Irene Eber, Richard Elphick, Stewart Gillmor, Oliver Holmes, Jerome Long, Donald Meyer, Ronald Schatz, Richard Slotkin, David Swift, Frank B. Tipton, Jr., and Stephen White. These good people at various times have borne with my eccentric opinions. At crucial steps in the manuscript preparation, Bill Dillon, Edna Haran, Sharon Rasmussen, Melissa Totten, and Joseph Urgo have helped me. Finally, I would like to express my appreciation to Professor Leon F. Litwack, who directed this study as a dissertation and then read numerous drafts of the book manuscript. In his work both as a teacher and scholar he has established high standards for me and his other students to follow.

A Rock in a Weary Land

Introduction

Most studies of black religion in the eighteenth and nineteenth centuries have either traced the origins of the independent black churches or analyzed the theology of slave religion. These works suggest that black people, slave and free, created under trying circumstances a rich and varied religious life that gave them strength and solace during their travail.[1] Although *A Rock in a Weary Land* draws on this scholarship, its primary concern is with the missionary work of the African Methodist Episcopal Church in the South during and after the Civil War. It focuses specifically on the organizational and political difficulties that the church encountered while working with the freedmen. In exploring these problems, I have paid attention to the religious goals of the A.M.E. Church, but theology is not the main subject of my study.

For Methodists, religion was more than a ritualistic exercise: they believed that conversion brought the converted into close association with God. Once this was accomplished, it was the duty of the saved to bring God's word to the unredeemed. Operating on these assumptions, the clergy and laity of the A.M.E. Church believed it was their duty to bring the message of God's love and the promise of salvation to America's poor, disadvantaged, and sinful blacks. These ideas provided eighteenth- and nineteenth-century black Methodists with a common belief system that

---

1. Carol George, *Segregated Sabbaths* (New York: Oxford University Press, 1973); Lawrence W. Levine, *Black Culture and Black Consciousness* (New York: Oxford University Press, 1977), 5–80; Albert Raboteau, *Slave Religion: The Invisible Institution in the Antebellum South* (New York: Oxford University Press, 1978).

enabled them to connect their temporal and spiritual lives to the civil order.[2]

The church's mission to the slaves was a specific version of American "civil religion" in the nineteenth century—that is, the carrying out of God's will on earth. Most evangelical Protestants, black and white, in the nineteenth century believed that history was progressive and that God was history's prime mover. They also thought of themselves as being elect, chosen, and covenanted with God to effect his purposes for the world. Although blacks and whites shared a common belief system, they used the system for different purposes. White Americans used it to conquer a continent and demonstrate America's providential role in the history of mankind. Their black fellow countrymen used it to "elevate the race," that is, to Christianize and improve the economic and social position of their people in American society. The A.M.E. Church's mission to the slaves, then, was both spiritual and temporal. Not only were souls to be saved but productive and loyal citizens were to be created.[3]

In undertaking this endeavor, A.M.E. missionaries believed that they were instruments of God's will, that God had given their church a special task—to uplift the black race in America and then in the world. To these people the Civil War represented a watershed in the history of the Republic. The destruction of slavery was God's punishment on America for the sin of slavery. The peculiar institution had prevented the United States from realizing its democratic ideal. Although the destruction of Negro bondage was inevitable (because God willed it), this did not mean that the black man should be idle; he had a duty to participate in his liberation. This task could not be left in the hands of white men, for it would make black freedmen a product of white charity. Imbued with a sense of mission, A.M.E. missionaries went south to elevate the freed-

2. Harry V. Richardson, *Dark Salvation* (Garden City: Anchor Press/Doubleday, 1976), 11. For a definition of common belief system see Philip E. Converse, "The Nature of Belief System in Mass Publics," in David E. Apter (ed.), *Ideology and Discontent* (New York: The Free Press, 1964), 207.

3. For the concept "civil religion" see Robert N. Bellah, *Beyond Belief: Essays on Religion in a Post Traditional World* (New York: Harper and Row, 1970), 168–89; Leonard I. Sweet, *Black Images of America, 1784–1870.* (New York: W. W. Norton, 1976), Ch. 5. For this idea in black thought see Frederick Cooper, "Elevating the Race: The Social Thought of Black Leaders, 1827–1850," *American Quarterly*, XXIV (December, 1972), 604–26.

men. Their success was mixed. A variety of forces internal and external prevented them from achieving all of their goals.

This study argues that Methodism operating as a common belief system provided the rationale for the creation of a black middle class. Specifically, the founders of the A.M.E. Church believed that Methodism's discipline would transform the lives of their people and make them useful and productive members of American society. This racial ideology, if I may borrow a phrase from *Negro Thought in America*, precedes the efforts described in August Meier's superb book. Following the lead of Meier and others, *A Rock in a Weary Land* not only establishes certain continuities in black thought; it also demonstrates that black religion was not an opiate. In fact, in certain instances the church provided an arena for the politization of the freedmen.[4]

It has been my special concern in telling the story of the A.M.E. Church's mission to the freedmen to focus on those issues that were important to the church. The primary concern of the A.M.E. Church, as this study shows, was the black Methodist. Thus, those readers who might be interested, for example, in A.M.E. relations with the black Baptist in the South will find no discussion of that topic here. A recent study of that denomination, during the Civil War and Reconstruction, suggests that the black Baptists were primarily concerned with putting their own house in order. Absorbed by internal problems, the black Baptists were not interested in the missionary work of the A.M.E. Church.[5]

4. August Meier, *Negro Thought in America, 1880–1915* (Ann Arbor: University of Michigan Press, 1963); Jane H. Pease and William H. Pease, *They Who Would Be Free* (New York, Atheneum, 1974), 95–171.
5. For a discussion of this problem see James Melvin Washington, "The Origins and Emergence of Black Baptist Separatism, 1863–1897" (Ph.D. dissertation, Yale University, 1979), 45–155.

I A Way Out: Richard Allen and the Founding of the A.M.E. Church

The Civil War and Reconstruction gave northern free Negro religious organizations an opportunity long denied them: the chance to work with their formerly enslaved brethren. The African Methodist Episcopal Church was the first black religious institution to send missionaries south, and the church's assumption of this vanguard position was consistent with its early history as a champion of Negro rights in antebellum America.

1 Organized on April 9, 1816, by a group of northern free blacks led by Richard Allen, the A.M.E. Church grew out of a racial dispute that disrupted the congregation of St. George's Methodist Episcopal Church in Philadelphia. The disturbance occurred in November of 1792 when black members of the congregation were forced out of seats they had taken in the church's gallery. This incident was the culminating event in a series of such occurrences that had marred St. George's services since blacks began to worship there in large numbers at Richard Allen's urging. Allen and his followers left the church and never returned.[1]

1. The standard biography of Richard Allen is Charles H. Wesley, *Richard Allen: Apostle of Freedom* (Washington: Associated Publishers, 1935). For a more recent study of Allen's life and career, see Carol George, *Segregated Sabbaths* (New York: Oxford University Press, 1973). Both of these works draw on, in some way or another, Richard Allen's autobiography, *The Life Experience and Gospel Labors of the Rt. Rev. Richard Allen to which is annexed the Rise and Progress of the African Methodist Episcopal Church in the United States of America* (Nashville: A.M.E. School Union, n.d.). This volume also includes "The African Supplement" and "A Narrative of the Yellow Fever in the Year of Our Lord 1793," which Allen coauthored with his friend Absalom Jones, as well as three short pamphlets by Allen: "An Address to the People of Color," "A Short

After Allen and his band withdrew from St. George's they focused their energies on the self-help organization called the Free African Society which they had established in 1787. The society became a substitute for a church, but the program which it adopted was not to Allen's liking. Ultimately Allen, who wanted to organize a black Methodist church, left the Free African Society. His departure reflected his belief that Methodism was the religious system best suited to the needs of black people. "I was confident," Allen wrote, "that there was no religious sect or denomination which would suit the capacity of the colored people as well as the Methodist; for this plain and simple gospel suits best for any people; for the unlearned can understand, and the learned are sure to understand; and the reason that the Methodist [are] so successful [in] the awakening and conversion of the colored people, [is their] plain doctrine and . . . good discipline."[2]

John Wesley, the father of Methodism, preached a simple doctrine which emphasized the importance of conversion experience. To be admitted to a Methodist society, a prospective member had to undergo a conversion during which he was reborn and delivered from sin. He would experience, through the operation of the Holy Spirit, the presence of God, be forgiven for his sins, and assured salvation. To help followers exemplify their salvation, Wesley wrote the *General Rules* or *Discipline*, which outlined a guide to Christian ethics. The *General Rules* included prohibitions against swearing, fighting, drinking, sabbath breaking, gossiping, failing to pay debts, attending the theater, and engaging in the slave trade. Methodists were also required to be "plain in speech and dress" and to intermarry. The aim of these regulations was to set the Methodists apart, as the Quakers were. Entrance to a Methodist society was fairly

---

Address to the Friends of Him Who Hath No Helper," and "An Address to Those Who Keep Slaves and Approve the Practice." The following discussion of Allen's life and ideas is taken from *The Life Experience and Gospel Labors of the Rt. Rev. Richard Allen* unless otherwise cited, pp. 7–24. Milton C. Sernett's recent study *Black Religion and American Evangelicalism, 1787–1865* (New Jersey: The Scarecrow Press, Inc., and The American Theological Library Association, 1975), revises Allen's autobiography with respect to the year in which the blacks seceded from St. George's. The secession, Sernett says, occurred in 1792 rather than 1787. See page 117 and footnotes 24 and 25 in Chapter 5 of this fine book.

2. Quoted in Wesley, *Richard Allen*, 71–72. This study also contains a discussion of Allen's reasons for leaving the Free African Society, 59–72. For the rules of the Free African Society, see Benjamin T. Tanner, *An Outline of Our History and Government for African Methodist Churchmen* (Philadelphia: A.M.E. Book Concern, 1884), 140–141.

easy. It was only after a person had been admitted and received his class ticket that this discipline began to affect his life.[3]

Wesley conceived of Methodism as a means of fellowship. He believed that the members of his church should be united to "help each other work out their salvation." "In fellowship," Wesley thought, "strength would be gained, and the feeble and lonely would be sheltered and cheered." Within Methodism there were three organized units of fellowship: the class, the society, and the band. There was no prescribed chronology for the organization of these units. Usually a class was formed first, then a society, and later on bands. Bands were smaller units within the class or classes.

The class was the most significant of the three units. Every Methodist society was composed of several classes. In some places, a class was organized before a society. Members were required to attend class meetings regularly and non-attendance was grounds for expulsion from the society. In every class an attendance roll was kept by the class leader. On the roll the attendance record of members was marked *A*, *P*, or *D*—absent, present, or distant. Admission to class during the early years of Methodism was by ticket only. The ticket was renewed quarterly by the preacher, but if a member was delinquent, it was withheld.

The importance of the class may be found in both the discipline and the training it provided its members. A class consisted of a small group of Christians, usually not more than twelve, who met regularly for Christian fellowship under the guidance of a class leader. Members were expected to contribute one penny a week in dues and participate in devotions. The experience of meeting in classes deeply affected the people who became Methodists.[4]

Several British historians, most notably E. P. Thompson, have pointed out the far-reaching influence Methodism exerted on the English working class in the eighteenth and nineteenth centuries. Methodism's fervent message, hierarchical structure, religious services, weekly class meetings,

---

3. Wade Crawford Barclay, *To Reform the Nation* (New York: The Board of Missions and Church Extension of the Methodist Church, 1950), Vol. II of *Early American Methodist, 1769–1844*, 303. See *The Doctrine and Discipline of the Methodist Episcopal Church* (20th ed.; New York: N. Bangs and T. Mason Publisher, 1820); Barclay, *To Reform the Nation*, 349. On the subject of Methodism and slavery, see Donald Mathews, *Slavery and Methodism* (Princeton: Princeton University Press, 1965) and Robert Southey, *The Life of Wesley and the Rise and Progress of Methodism*, ed. J. Atkinson (New York: Frederick Warne Co., 1889), 503.
4. Barclay, *To Reform the Nation*, 337–39.

and love feasts taught the English working class the importance of education, hard work, sexual restraint, and abstinence from liquor. At the same time they learned how "to combine in associations, to make rules for their own governance, to raise funds and to communicate from one part of the kingdom to another." Based on his own life and experience, Richard Allen believed that Methodism would do the same for black people in America. Stated another way, what Allen wanted his church to do was instill the Yankee virtues of industry, thrift, and self-reliance. This Allen believed would be accomplished by getting black people to adhere to Methodist discipline. The church, in short, would be the agency in which the Negro's "character" was shaped or formed. A.M.E. missionaries, this study will suggest, tried to accomplish this goal when they began working with the freedmen during the Civil War and Reconstruction.[5]

Allen had been born a slave but through hard work and thrift he had been able to purchase his freedom and amass a sizable fortune. After he arrived in Philadelphia in 1786, he had worked as a shoemaker employing several journeymen and apprentices. He also had run a chimney sweep business which employed several boys. With the profits from these enterprises, he had been able to purchase several pieces of property. When he died in 1830 his estate was appraised at $40,000, not including his personal "goods," "chattels," and "credits" which executors estimated to be worth $3,983.17. Allen's financial success was a truly remarkable achievement at a time when few white men left such large estates and when the majority of free blacks lived in dire poverty. Allen's wealth did not blind him to the conditions in which most black people lived. Having been "born and awakened" under the Methodists, he attributed his success in life to them. The Methodists had taught him that lower-class people had possibilities within themselves for moral improvement and personal achievement. In an age when the lower classes were generally despised and thought helpless—by themselves and by their detractors—Wesley preached that every man was inherently good and that it was possible

5. Quoted in E. P. Thompson, *The Making of the English Working Class* (New York: Vintage Books, 1963), 42. See also E. R. Taylor, *Methodism and Politics, 1791–1815* (Cambridge: Cambridge University Press, 1935); Robert Wearmouth, *Methodism and the Working Class Movements of England, 1800–1850* (London: Epworth Press, 1937). Thompson's thesis that Methodism in some sense defused the revolutionary potential inherent in the English working classes does not hold in the case of the A.M.E. Church. The political thrust of the A.M.E. Church remained strong despite the potential consequences of Methodist doctrine. (See Chapter V herein.)

with God's grace to lead a life of purity and holiness. To a person accustomed to a life of hopelessness and subordination, Wesley's message offered a way out.[6]

By 1794 Richard Allen was ready to help those black people who were willing to follow him and accept Wesley's message. Since his departure from the Free African Society he had gathered a small band of followers. On May 5, 1794, Allen's followers assembled at his house "in order to consult together upon the best and most eligible means to provide for ourselves a house to meet in for religious worship agreeable to our desires, according to the light God through grace has given us—separate from our white brethren."[7] This meeting led to the organization of the Bethel African Methodist Episcopal Church.

When Allen organized his church he did not give much thought to what the relationship of Bethel would be to the Methodist Episcopal Church. The question of who was to run the church was not settled. Preachers were sent to Bethel by the elder of St. George's Methodist Episcopal Church, but title to the church was held by the black trustees. This division of authority led to a conflict which was to last for twenty-two years. The difficulties between the Allenites and the white Methodists were resolved in 1816 when the supreme court of Pennsylvania declared Bethel to be an independent church.[8]

From 1794 to 1816 the church struggled for its independence. The issues which divided the Bethelites and their white co-religionists provide an interesting insight into the development of American race relations after the Revolution. When viewed in a broader context, the persistent

6. Wesley, *Richard Allen*, 76, 225. The plight of northern free Negroes is discussed in Leon F. Litwack, *North of Slavery* (Chicago: University of Chicago Press, 1961), 2–4; Wade Crawford Barclay, *Missionary Motivation and Expansion*, Vol. I of *Early American Methodism, 1769–1844*, xxiv.
7. Quoted in Wesley, *Richard Allen*, 77.
8. For details of this struggle the following works should be consulted: *Articles of Association of the African Methodist Episcopal Church of the City of Philadelphia in the Commonwealth of Pennsylvania* (1799; reprinted Afro-American History Series, Maxwell Whitman (ed.), Philadelphia: RHistoric Publications, No. 201, 1969). See also "African Supplement" in *The Life Experience and Gospel Labors of the Rt. Rev. Richard Allen*, 24–28. See Robert Burch's statement, December 16, 1815. For the white Methodist reaction to the Allenites' assertion of independence, see the letters by J. Emory to St. George's Church and Bethel African Methodist Episcopal Church, April 6, 1815; Samuel Shoemaker to Bethel African Methodist Episcopal Church, April 7, 1815; and Joseph Hopkinson to Bethel African Methodist Episcopal Church, April 24, 1815, all in Edward Carey Gardiner Collection, Box 33, Pennsylvania Historical Society, Philadelphia.

harassment of Bethel by the elders of the Methodist Church suggests more than a desire to win lawsuits. It was part of a general effort on the part of whites to reassert control over blacks—a control which they thought they had lost in the wake of the Revolution. To the white Methodists, Bethel represented a form of Negro assertion which they could not tolerate. The church's existence was a comment on their failure as Christians. They had raised the bar of caste in the House of God and forced the blacks out.

To propagate his ideas about Methodism, Allen needed an organization with disciples located around the country. Events in Baltimore, New York, and several other northern cities would provide him with both an organization and followers. The religious difficulties which Allen and his followers experienced in Philadelphia were repeated in several other American cities. "About this time," Allen writes, "our colored friends in Baltimore were treated in a similar manner by the white preachers and trustees, and many of them driven away who were disposed to seek a place of worship rather than go to law." With blacks elsewhere facing a similar proscription, Allen decided in April, 1816, to call a general conference.[9]

Sixteen delegates assembled in Philadelphia on April 9, 1816. They came from Baltimore, Maryland; Wilmington, Delaware; Attleborough, Pennsylvania; Salem, New Jersey; and Philadelphia. They resolved to unify as the African Methodist Episcopal Church. "We demanded it expedient," the resolution said, "to have a form of discipline, whereby we may guide our people in the fear of God." Referring to their white co-religionists, the delegates vowed to preserve themselves "from that spiritual despotism which we have so recently experienced—remembering that we are not to lord it over God's heritage, as greedy dogs that can never have enough."[10]

By 1816, this attitude was shared by a number of black people. They

---

9. For the organization of African Methodism these works should be consulted: Emory Stevens Bucke (ed.), *The History of American Methodism* (3 vols.; New York: Abingdon Press, 1964), I, 603–606 and II, 536–39; Mason Crum, *The Negro in the Methodist Church* (New York: Editorial Department Division of Education and Cultivation Board of Missions and Church Extension of the Methodist Church, 1951); George, *Segregated Sabbaths*; Joseph C. Hartzell, "Methodism and the Negro in the United States," *Journal of Negro History*, VIII (July, 1923), 301–15; J. F. Shaw, *The Negro in the History of Methodism* (Nashville: Parthenon Press, 1954).
10. *The Life Experience and Gospel Labors of the Rt. Rev. Richard Allen*, 24.

saw their white brothers as being proud and avaricious. These two faults had made the whites insensitive to the blacks' aspirations. To preserve themselves from these vices, the blacks deemed it necessary to found a new church and thereby rekindle the spiritual flame which the white Methodists had extinguished. In short, they were revitalizing Methodism, after it had grown cold and become insensitive to the needs of some of its adherents. The blacks were returning to what Allen called "the good old way, and desired to walk therein."

The church that Allen and his associates organized adopted the Discipline of the Methodist Episcopal Church with only a few minor changes. The pro-slavery provisions in the Methodist Discipline were stricken out, and the office of presiding elder was abolished in the A.M.E. hierarchy. After the Civil War this office would be reinstituted "in such of the annual conferences as chose to adopt it." Believing it was necessary that someone should supervise their church, the delegates, on April 9, 1816, held elections for the office of bishop. The Reverend Daniel Coker was elected but he resigned the next day in an action never fully explained. After Coker's resignation, Richard Allen was elected bishop on April 11, 1816. He was duly consecrated by the prayers and laying on of hands of five ordained ministers, one of whom was his friend Absalom Jones, an ordained minister of the Protestant Episcopal Church.[11]

11. For this tendency (revitalization) in Protestant movements, see Richard H. Niebuhr's essay, "The Protestant Movement and Democracy in the United States," in James Ward Smith and A. Leland Jamison, eds., *The Shaping of American Religion* (Princeton: Princeton University Press, 1961), 20–71; Carl M. Tanner, *Reprint of the First Edition of the Discipline of the A.M.E. Church, with a Historical Preface and Notes* (1817; reprinted Atlanta: n.p., 1917); see also Jabez P. Campbell, "Our Episcopacy," *A.M.E. Review*, VI (July, 1889), 2–3; Tanner, *An Outline of Our History and Government for African Methodist Churchmen*, 71. Coker's resignation is clouded in mystery and historians have advanced various reasons for his resignation. Ira Berlin, in *Slaves Without Masters* (New York: Pantheon Books, 1974), 281, argues that Coker, who was light skinned, was forced to resign because the darker members of the church wanted a bishop who resembled them. Carol George in *Segregated Sabbaths* also cites color as a possible reason for Coker's resignation. She also suggests that Coker's interest in colonization may have caused him to resign. Wesley, in *Richard Allen*, 151–53, questions the source that both Berlin and George use to argue that Coker resigned because of his color. Finally, a fourth interpretation of the resignation is given by Campbell in his essay "Our Episcopacy." For these events see Wesley, *Richard Allen*, 154–55. As the first bishop of the A.M.E. Church, Allen was "primus inter pares" among the church's elders. His Episcopacy did not rest on the claim of apostolic succession and was distinguished by some other characteristics peculiar to the A.M.E. Church. First, the office of bishop in the A.M.E. Church was general, not diocesan. The authority of the church's bishops extended throughout the church and was not limited to one diocese or district. Second,

The church was called the African Methodist Episcopal Church because this was the term used to denominate blacks in the eighteenth and
early nineteenth centuries. It did not mean, as one A.M.E. minister explained, "Methodism Africanized, nor Methodism from or for Africans
only." He wrote, "The term expresses no fact as to accident of birth nor
geographical position, yet it is significant in an ethnological sense. It
expresses the fact that the church was founded, controlled by, and chief-
ly composed of persons of African descent, with African blood in their
veins." The creation of this church constituted the fulfillment of a dream
that Richard Allen had held since 1786. There now existed in America a
church run and controlled by black people, one dedicated to improving
their condition.[12]

2   An examination of the prewar history of the church reveals the tradition of public service that A.M.E. missionaries brought with them to the
South. Believing that black people were citizens and that citizenship en-
tailed both rights and obligations, Allen and his friends on several occasions offered their services to the city of Philadelphia. In 1793, when Philadelphia was swept by a yellow fever epidemic, Allen and Absalom Jones
organized a group of black people to help the sick and bury the dead.
During the War of 1812, Allen, Jones, and James Forten, a wealthy black
sail maker who lived in Philadelphia, organized a troop of black men to
help defend the city. The goal of these efforts on the part of Allen and his
friends was two-fold. First, they wanted to instill in the black people of
Philadelphia a sense of civic pride. They wanted them to see that the city
was as much theirs as it was white people's, that blacks as citizens of Philadelphia were also responsible for the tenor of life in the city. Second,

---

the bishops were itinerant rather than stationary and holders of the office were required
to travel throughout the connection. "Thus, Richard Allen was Bishop of the whole
church, and travelled wherever the church was." In 1852 three of Allen's successors
changed this system and formed a bishop's council. They divided the church into three
episcopal districts, each of which was presided over by a bishop, and used the council
to exercise the general superintendency. For the history of A.M.E. bishops, see Richard
R. Wright, Jr., *The Bishops of the A.M.E. Church* (Nashville: A.M.E. Sunday School
Union, 1963), 22–23.

12. Wesley, *Richard Allen*, 81. John T. Jenifer, "What Has African Methodism To Say as to
Its Past? What Has It To Offer the Present? What Does It Promise the Future?" *A.M.E.
Review*, III (July, 1884), 254.

they desired to improve relations between blacks and whites in the city.[13]

In a series of short articles Allen addressed himself to the question of black and white relations. Having been born a slave, Allen was well acquainted with the master-slave relationship. In an article entitled "An Address to Those Who Keep Slaves and Approve the Practice," he asked slaveholders to try the following experiment: "We believe if you would try the experiment of taking a few black children, and cultivate their minds with the same care and let them have the same prospect in view as to living in the world, as you would wish for your own children, you would find upon trial they were not inferior in mental endowments." Allen was telling the slaveholders that black people were not innately suited for slavery, and that slavery and slave behavior were products of conditioning, not of color. Allen said he did not wish to make the slaveholders angry, but only wanted them to consider "how hateful slavery [was] in the sight of God." In prophetic words, he concluded: "If you love your children, if you love your country . . . clear your hands from slaves; burden not your children or your country with them."[14]

Allen's personal experience deeply influenced his thoughts about slavery. He had been an exceptional slave with an exceptional master. To slaves with kind masters he wrote: "You may put your trust in God, who sees your condition, and as a merciful father pitieth his children, so doth God pity them that love Him; and as your hearts are inclined to serve God, you will feel an affectionate reward [sic] toward your masters and mistresses, so-called, and the whole family in which you live. This will be seen by them and tend to promote your liberty, especially with such as have feeling masters." His advice to the less fortunate was: "You will have the favor of God dwelling in your hearts which you will value more than anything else, which will be a consolation in the worst condition you can be in and [your] master [cannot] deprive you of it." The ideas of forgiveness and reconciliation appear over and over again in Allen's writing. "To you who are favored with freedom," Allen wrote, "let your conduct manifest your gratitude toward the compassionate masters who have set you free; and let no rancor or ill-will lodge in your breast for any bad treatment you may have received."[15]

13. "A Narrative of the Proceedings of the Colored People During the Awful Calamity in Philadelphia in the Year 1793," in *The Life Experience and Gospel Labors of the Rt. Rev. Richard Allen,* 31–46; Wesley, *Richard Allen,* 145–46.
14. *The Life Experience and Gospel Labors of the Rt. Rev. Richard Allen,* 49–50.
15. *Ibid.,* 51–52.

Allen asked black people to be strong in their Christian faith. The strength which they derived from Christianity would allow them to see the spiritual weakness of their oppressors. From this perception would come a sense of spiritual superiority which would prevent the slaves and free Negroes from falling into self-rejecting rage. To illustrate the importance of forgiveness, reconciliation, and harmony, Allen published a pamphlet in 1808 in which he described what happened to black people who lacked a sense of self-worth and discipline. In 1808, two black men, John Joyce, alias Davis, and his friend Peter Matthias, alias Mathews, murdered Mrs. Sarah Cross, a white storekeeper in Philadephia. The men were tried, found guilty, and condemned to death. To show the black people of the city what to him was the moral lesson of such lives, Allen published Joyce's and Matthias's confessions, under the title "Address to the Public and People of Colour, in the confession of John Joyce, alias Davis, who was executed on Monday, the 14th of March 1808, for the murder of Mrs. Sarah Cross; with an address to the Public and People of Colour, together with the substance of the trial and Chief Justice Tilgham on his condemnation." The lesson was that crime and dissipation did not pay; moreover, to lead such a life was to accept white society's definition of blacks as being degenerate. It was also a betrayal of duty. Allen believed free black people had a mission in America. "Much depends upon us," he wrote, "for the help of our color—more than many are aware. If we are lazy and idle, the enemies of freedom plead it as a cause why we ought not to be free, and say we are better in a state of servitude, and that giving us our liberty would be an injury to us; . . . by such conduct we strengthen the bonds of oppression and keep many in bondage who are more worthy than ourselves."[16]

In the ideas of Allen and the founders of the A.M.E. Church can be seen the origins of that philosophy of self-help that American historians traditionally associate with Booker T. Washington. The emphasis which these men placed on self-help grew out of their awareness of the plight of the free Negro in antebellum northern society. Cut off from most social services, free blacks needed an institution that would serve as a center for community life; a place where they could worship, meet socially, and ed-

16. *Confessions of John Joyce, alias Davis, who was Executed on Monday the 14th of March, 1808, For the Murder of Mrs. Sarah Cross, with an Address to the Public and People of Colour, Together with the substance of the Trial, and the Address of Chief Justice Tilghman, on His Condemnation* (Philadelphia: printed at No. 12 Walnut Street, 1808). This pamphlet also contains *The Confession of Peter Matthias, Alias Mathews.*

ucate their children. Such a place was provided for free blacks by the A.M.E. Church and it served as the fixed point from which church members drew their strength. Members of this church lived their lives in accordance with the Methodist Discipline; they were to be thrifty, sober, neat, and hard-working. Those members of the church who prospered were enjoined to practice Christian charity. "In its nature," Allen wrote of Christian charity, "it is pure and disinterested, remote from all hopes or views of worldly return or recompense from the persons we relieve. We are to do good and lend, hoping for nothing again."[17]

Wealth and prosperity brought with them certain responsibilities, Allen taught his followers. They were to apply some part of their "substance," the product of their labors, "towards the relief and support of the poor and needy." While doing this they were to remember that God "had not committed his goods to us as dead stock, to be boarded up, or to lie unprofitably in our own hands. He expects that we shall put them out to proper and beneficial uses, and raise them to an advanced value by doing good with them as often as we have opportunity of laying them out upon the real interest and welfare of his poor children." One of the ways A.M.E. members were urged to use their money was to support education.[18]

In 1796 Allen and the trustees of Bethel established a free school to give the children and adults of the church reading lessons. "No man in his day was a greater lover of education than he. Whenever he could hear of a young man going to college or to any high school, he would send him a word of encouragement if not some money to sustain him." To provide his followers with educational materials, Allen organized, in 1817, the Book Concern of the A.M.E. Church. This publishing house was incorporated in 1855 under the laws of the state of Pennsylvania and published the Doctrine and Discipline of the A.M.E. Church, the church's hymnal, and other literature.[19]

Throughout the nineteenth century, the conferences of the A.M.E. Church passed resolutions on education. In 1833 the Ohio Conference

17. Tanner, *Reprint of the First Edition of the Discipline of A.M.E. Church*; *The Life Experience and Gospel Labors of the Rt. Rev. Richard Allen*, 55.
18. The Life Experience and Gospel Labors of the Rt. Rev. Richard Allen, 56.
19. Benjamin W. Arnett (ed.), *The Budget* (Xenia: Torchlight Printing Co., 1881), 149, quoted in Benjamin T. Tanner, *An Apology for African Methodism* (Baltimore: Methodist Episcopal Book Concern, 1883), 94; Wright, *The Bishops of the A.M.E. Church*, 32.

resolved "that common schools, Sunday Schools, and temperance societies are the highest importance to all people; but more especially to us as a people . . . it shall be the duty of every member of this conference to do all in his power to promote and establish these useful institutions among our people." In 1848 the General Conference of the church resolved "that each pastor of each principal church in the cities, establish a High School for the education of the rising generation." Although resolutions such as these were passed at a number of A.M.E. conferences before the Civil War, very little else was done, probably because of a lack of money.[20]

In 1848 the church acquired a newspaper, the *Christian Herald*. Four years later the name was changed to the *Christian Recorder*. The masthead of this paper read: "The Christian Recorder Published by the African Methodist Episcopal Church in the United States, for the Dissemination of Religion, Morality, Literature, and Science." In 1863 the church acquired its own university and named it Wilberforce after the famous British abolitionist.[21]

Through its newspaper, university, and publishing house, the church inculcated its members with a sense of mission. The A.M.E. Church was an instrument of God's providence. Members of the church believed that God had raised up their church "to minister in holy things: first and foremost to the Anglo-Africans upon this continent, and then to the colored races of the earth." To make this belief a reality, members of the church were to be examples of self-help and uplift. It was believed that self-help and uplift would do two things for black people. First, black people who were not members of the church would emulate the middle class behavior of church members; also, it was hoped that nonmembers would be inspired to join. The church would thus provide a positive image for blacks and counteract the opinion of many whites that all Negroes were lazy and uncultured. Second, it was hoped that the image of success and morality provided by church members would dispel the web of prejudice and hatred which surrounded black people in America. A sense of mission set the A.M.E. Church off from other groups of black Christians. The clergy and laity of the church saw themselves as agents of God for

20. Quoted in Grace Naomi Perry, "The Educational Work of the A.M.E. Church Prior to 1900" (M.A. thesis, Howard University, 1948), 15–16; Arnett, *The Budget*, 170; Perry, "The Educational Work of the A.M.E. Church Prior to 1900," 22.
21. Daniel Alexander Payne, *Recollections of Seventy Years* (1888; reprinted New York: Arno Press and New York *Times*, 1969), 153.

the task of elevating the Negro race in America—a task they thought was
theirs because they were Methodist and black. Later this conflation of
ethnicity and religion created serious difficulties for the A.M.E. Church.[22]

The church's assumption of a vanguard position in the black community meant that A.M.E. ministers had to do more than just preach. They
had to minister to both the spiritual and temporal needs of their congregations. As the career of Richard Allen indicates, black ministers provided a number of services which normally would have been performed
by a professional class, but because the black community was poor and
illiterate its ministers filled this void in community life. The esteem in
which they were held and their literacy enabled these black clergymen to
mold and galvanize opinion in their flocks. Certainly this was the case
when African colonization became an issue in the black community.

The church's sense of mission caused it to oppose the plans of the American Colonization Society. Founded in 1817 as a benevolent aid association, it proposed to transport free Negroes to the west coast of Africa
where they would work to redeem their African brothers. The goals of
the society were not totally benevolent. Members of the society wished to
remove free Negroes from America because they considered them to be
fractious, degraded, alien, and unassimilable. This program of Negro removal clashed with the mission of the A.M.E. Church and threatened to
deprive it of prospective members. If a large number of Negroes accepted
the society's offer of colonization in Africa, the church's program of disciplined development in America would be undercut. Initially Allen and
his friend James Forten favored some form of Negro emigration to Africa. But when the A.C.S. became an advocate of Negro removal, Allen
and Forten changed their position and came to view it as another example of white coercion. In January, 1817, a number of prominent Philadelphia Negroes met in convention to protest the plans of the A.C.S.
Allen, Jones, and Forten participated but did not reveal their coloniza-
tionist sympathies. The convention met in Bethel Church, protested the
colonizers' assertion that free Negroes were unassimilable, noted that Negroes were among the first settlers of America, and vowed not to leave the
country.[23]

22. *Christian Recorder*, March 26, 1864.
23. George M. Fredrickson, *The Black Image in the White Mind: The Debate on Afro-
American Character and Destiny, 1817–1914* (New York: Harper and Row, 1971),

Colonization continued to be debated in the black communities of America. In a letter to *Freedom's Journal* on November 2, 1827, Allen criticized the movement. "I have for several years been striving to reconcile my mind to the colonization of Africans in Liberia," Allen wrote, "but there have always been, and there still remain great and insurmountable objections against the scheme. We are an unlettered people, brought up in ignorance; not one in a thousand has a liberal education. Is there any fitness for such to be sent into a far country, among heathens, to convert or civilize them, when they themselves are neither civilized or Christianized?" Allen then asked his readers to look at "the great bulk of . . . poor ignorant Africans in this country; exposed to every temptation before them; for the want of their morals being refined by education."[24]

Colonization, Allen continued, was a slaveholders' plot. "Can we not discern the project of sending the free people of color away from this country? Is it not for the interest of the slaveholder to select the free people of color out of the different states and send them to Liberia? Will it not make their slaves uneasy to see free men of color enjoying liberty?" Free men of color, therefore, should stay in America. In a society in which it was argued that their natural condition was a state of thralldom, free black people, by their presence, undermined the institution of slavery. They were anomalies which the slaveholder could not explain and therefore chose to send away.[25]

America was the black man's country also, Allen told his readers. It was their country because they had helped to build it: "We were stolen from our mother country and brought here, we have tilled the ground and made fortunes for thousands, and still they are not weary of our services." What the slaveholders wanted, though, was the service of slaves and not those of free blacks. Allen concluded his letter by asking a series of questions. "Is there not land enough in America, or corn enough in Egypt? Why should free Negroes be sent away to die? When thousands of foreigners are immigrating to America every year? If there [was] . . . ground sufficient for them to cultivate and bread for them to eat why

---

8–10; George, *Segregated Sabbaths*, 152; William Lloyd Garrison, *Thoughts on African Colonization* (1832; reprinted Arno Press and New York *Times*, 1968), 1–10; Wesley, *Richard Allen*, 161.
24. *Freedom's Journal*, November 2, 1827.
25. *Ibid.*

would they insist to send the tillers of the soil away? Africans have made fortunes for thousands who are yet unwilling to part with their services, but the free must be sent away and those who remain must be slave?" Finally, he averred, "this land, which we have watered with our tears and our blood is now our mother country: and we are well satisfied to stay where wisdom abounds and Gospel is free."[26] Three years later Allen would modify his position on colonization.

In 1830 a number of free Negroes assembled in Philadelphia to discuss national questions which faced them. This convention was billed as a national meeting to differentiate it from the 1817 gathering, which had been a local affair. Richard Allen presided at the convention, which was called to deal with two questions: emigration to Canada and the work of the American Colonization Society.[27] On the question of Canadian emigration, the convention urged "the formation of a settlement in the British province of Upper Canada, [which] would be a great advantage to the people of colour." The members of the convention pledged their honor "to aid each other by all honourable means, to plant and support one [another] in that country." They "appealed" to their "colored brethern, and to all philanthropists here and elsewhere, to assist in this benevolent and important work." They chose Canada because no legal distinction of color was recognized there. "We shall be entitled to all the rights, privileges, and immunities of other citizens." Furthermore, in emigrating to Canada they would not have to learn a new language or suffer a dramatic change in weather. Finally, in Canada large numbers of black people would be able to work in occupations closed to them in America. They would be able to pursue both the mechanical and agricultural arts which would allow them to "expand and ennoble [their] minds." Richard Allen supported emigration to Canada because he thought the program of uplift he espoused could be implemented there. Allen and his followers were to be disappointed. The Canadian venture was to fail because of mismanagement, poor planning, and a lack of financial support.[28]

The convention closed with a statement against African colonization:

26. *Ibid.*
27. *Ibid.*
28. *Constitution of the American Society of Free Persons of Colour: For Improving Their Condition in the United States for Purchasing Lands; And for the Establishment of a Settlement in Upper Canada. Also the Proceedings of the Convention with Their Address to the Free Persons of Colour in the United States,* ed. Maxwell Whiteman (1831; reprinted Philadelphia: RHistoric Publications, No. 211, 1969), 10–11. For the failure

"However great the debt which these united may owe to injured Africa, and however unjustly her sons have been made to bleed, and her daughters to drink of the cup of affliction, still we who have been born and nurtured on this soil, we, whose habits, manners, and customs are the same in common with other Americans, can never consent to take our lives in our hands, and be the bearers of the redress by that society to that much afflicted country." Viewing Africa as a death trap, these black Americans chose to remain in the Western Hemisphere. They preferred to emigrate to Canada where the climate, soil, and people were similar to what they knew in the United States. Later on, after Richard Allen's death, the attitude of some members of his church toward Africa would change.[29]

3   Richard Allen died on March 26, 1831, at the age of seventy-two. The church which he founded in 1816 with only 400 members had spread throughout the North into New York and New England, and westward into Ohio. Precise membership figures for the A.M.E. Church during this period are difficult to find, and even the accounts of the founding of important congregations are often vague and contradictory. The available figures show that expansion was rapid, but expansion was fraught with problems arising from internal conflicts as well as external pressure. By 1836 it is estimated the church had a membership of 7,594 and was sending missionaries to Haiti. In 1840 it established a Canadian Conference and by 1856 it had conferences in Illinois, Indiana, Missouri, and Louisiana. The church by this time numbered some 20,000 souls. In some of the border states the church had difficulties expanding. In 1832, for example, Delaware would not allow A.M.E. ministers from non-slaveholding states to take charge of churches in that state. Because of this law, all of those appointed to go to Delaware that year were sent elsewhere. Prior to the Civil War, the A.M.E. Church was banned from the South by slaveholders who feared that it would serve as a catalyst for slave revolts.[30]

---

of Canadian emigration see Austin Steward, *Twenty Two Years a Slave and Forty Years a Freeman*, ed. Jane H. Pease and William H. Pease (1857; reprinted Reading: Addison Wesley, 1969).
29. *Constitution of the American Society of Free Persons of Colour*, 11.
30. Wright (ed.), *The Centennial Encyclopedia of the A.M.E. Church* (Philadelphia: Book Concern of the A.M.E. Church, 1916), 5. James A. Handy, *Scraps of African Methodist Episcopal History* (Philadelphia: A.M.E. Book Concern, n.d.), 110.

Despite its legal proscription, the A.M.E. Church did cross the Mason and Dixon line before the Civil War. "African Methodism was known to exist in the city of Mobile as early as 1820," Bishop Gaines claims, "but . . . the walls of slavery were towering high, therefore the little band had to bow low again." The establishment of the A.M.E. Church in Alabama is not documented, but it was probably founded by slaves from either Baltimore or Charleston who were resold via the slave trade. The church was not established again in Alabama until 1864. Before the Civil War, the two most conspicuous centers of African Methodism in the South were located in Charleston and New Orleans.[31]

The Charleston church dated from 1818, when a breach developed between the white and black Methodists of that city over control of a burial ground. Before this whites and blacks had worshiped together: "The galleries, hitherto crowded, were almost completely deserted," wrote a contemporary, "and it was a vacancy that could be felt. The absence of their responses and hearty songs were really felt to be a loss to those so long accustomed to hear them. . . . The Schismatics combined, and after great exertion succeeded in erecting a neat church building. . . . Their organization was called the African Church." In 1822 the church was forced to close because a number of its members were implicated in the Denmark Vesey plot.[32]

One of the leaders of this church was Morris Brown. Born on January 8, 1770, the son of mixed parents, Brown was converted to Methodism at an early age and, being a free man, he was able to secure a license to preach. In 1812 he started a movement to establish a free church for blacks in Charleston. On a trip to Philadelphia in 1816, he tried to have this church associated with the A.M.E. Church. However, this was not possible under the laws of South Carolina. In 1817 he was ordained a deacon and in 1818 he became an elder. Sometime before the Vesey conspiracy, he was jailed for a year for helping slaves to purchase their freedom. After the Vesey conspiracy became known, he was suspected as a participant and forced to flee. Reaching Philadelphia, he became, in 1825, the assistant pastor of Bethel. A year later he became the second bishop

31. Wesley J. Gaines, *African Methodism in the South or Twenty Five Years of Freedom* (Atlanta: Franklin Publishing House, 1890), 29; Bucke, *A History of American Methodism*, II, 537.
32. Quoted in U. B. Phillips, *American Negro Slavery* (1918: reprinted Baton Rouge: Louisiana State University Press, 1966), 420.

of the A.M.E. Church, and on Allen's death in 1831, Brown became presiding bishop.[33]

As for the church in New Orleans, it is difficult to discern exactly when it was founded. All that can be said with certainty is that sometime during the 1840s the A.M.E. Church established itself in New Orleans. After 1863 the A.M.E. Church would expand throughout the South. Itinerants of the church would bring the freedmen those ideas of order and discipline which Richard Allen cherished.[34]

The history of the church in the North before the Civil War suggests that Allen's ideas about discipline were not easily accepted by some of his followers. According to A.M.E. doctrine, the church was to be governed by the General Conference as the central policy-making board, but for two decades after the church was founded, the board could not claim its prerogatives. Why this state of affairs prevailed is difficult to say. Scattered evidence exists which suggests that the A.M.E. Church before and after the Civil War was torn by a great deal of infighting. Richard Allen's dream of a disciplined black church was slow in coming to fruition. For example, in 1843 the Baltimore Conference of the church was thrown into an uproar over a resolution requiring ministers to be able to read the Discipline and the Bible. This fight was symptomatic of a division which existed in the church between those who favored educating the clergy and those who did not.[35]

The principal advocate of ministerial education at this time was Daniel Alexander Payne. Payne was born in Charleston, South Carolina, on February 4, 1811. His parents were free Negroes "who made every sacrifice to educate him." When he was old enough to learn, his parents taught him to read and took him to Methodist class meetings. They died when he was quite young and Payne was raised by an aunt. After his parents' death, Payne continued his education with the help of the Brown Fellowship Society and the Minor Moralist Society. Both of these societies were run by free Negroes and were dedicated to educating free colored youth. The education Payne received in the societies' schools enabled him to study Latin, Greek, astronomy, history, and zoology on his own. He

33. Wright, *The Bishops of the A.M.E. Church*, 115–16.
34. Charles Spencer Smith, *A History of the A.M.E. Church* (Philadelphia: A.M.E. Book Concern, 1922), 34.
35. Bucke, *The History of American Methodism*, II, 538–39; Perry, "The Educational Work of the A.M.E. Church Prior to 1900," 22.

learned the carpenter's trade but soon left it to establish a school for colored children in Charleston. Payne ran his school from 1829 to 1835, when the authorities forced him to close.

Fleeing from South Carolina, he came north and enrolled in a Lutheran seminary. He was ordained a Lutheran minister in 1837 but left that church in 1840 and joined the A.M.E. Church. Payne's autobiography, *The Recollections of Seventy Years*, provides some interesting and colorful insights into nineteeth-century A.M.E. history. The attitudes of the clergy and members of the A.M.E. Church toward education, Payne recalls, caused him to join the Lutheran Church. "It was a common thing for the preachers of that church to introduce their sermons by declaring that they had 'not rubbed their heads against college walls,' at which the people would cry, 'Amen!'; they had 'never studied Latin or Greek,' at which the people would exclaim, 'Glory to God!'; they had 'never studied Hebrew,' at which all would 'shout.'" Later Payne would encounter these same prejudices.[36]

In 1850 Payne was assigned to the Ebenezer A.M.E. Church of Baltimore. "I went to Baltimore," Payne writes, "and in the evening met the class leaders and stewards, of whom I made inquiries concerning the condition of the charge: but to not one of my questions would they give any information. Therefore I said, 'Brethren, why do you not answer my questions?' The chief steward replied: 'Dr. Payne, we might as well tell you at once. The people met here last Wednesday and passed a resolution to reject you as their pastor.' Said I, 'Is this true?' He said, 'yes.' Then I rose, took my hat and cane, saying 'Goodbye, brethren; I shall never cross your threshold again as your pastor. But, said I, 'what are your reasons for refusing to have me as your pastor?' He said, 'the people say they have no objections to your moral character. They believe you are a Christian gentlemen; but they say you have too fine a carpet on your parlor floor, and you won't let them sing cornfield ditties, and if anyone of them should invite you to dine or take tea with him, you are too proud to do it.'"[37]

Although amusing, these disputes raise questions about the nature of

36. Wright, *The Bishops of the A.M.E. Church*, 266–67; Josephus R. Coan, *Daniel Alexander Payne Christian Educator* (Philadelphia: A.M.E. Book Concern, 1935); Payne, *Recollections of Seventy Years*, 64.
37. Payne, *History of the African Methodist Episcopal Church*, 3–4.

A.M.E. church services. That is, was worship in the church deeply influenced by either European Protestantism or African survivals, or was it a complex blend of both? Limited evidence suggests that some of the clergy and laity favored a blend of European and African religious forms. These people do not seem to have been satisfied by certain aspects of the church's liturgy. They found both the sermons and music of the A.M.E. Church inadequate to their spiritual needs. Some A.M.E. members, for example, did not approve of organs and choirs and considered them the devil's work. Other A.M.E. parishioners liked to perform ring shouts after church. Participants clapped their hands and stamped their feet until overcome by the power of the Holy Spirit. Falling to the ground, they would tremble or pass into catatonia. Upon being awakened, some celebrants would claim that they had been transported to heaven, where they had seen God and his angels. The music accompanying these rites was cornfield ditties—songs with lyrics like this:

> Ashes to ashes, dust to dust
> If God won't have us, the devil must.
>
> I was way over there where the coffin fell;
> I heard that sinner as he screamed in hell.

The presence of these rites in nineteenth-century A.M.E. churches suggests that not all of the Negroes' African cultural heritage disappeared in slavery. Indeed what is suggested is that this cultural heritage was appropriated to Christianity. Dance, song, and spirit possession made the scriptures come alive to these people—and a Christianity devoid of these practices would have been a dead religion to them. In some instances they were encouraged to behave this way by their ministers, who preached sermons which encouraged their congregations to shout.[38]

Religious services such as these created problems for A.M.E. clergymen, like Daniel Alexander Payne, who believed that their church should have educated ministers and dignified services. To Payne the rites described above were "ridiculous and heathenish," and did more harm than good, for they disgraced and corrupted black Christianity. What Payne favored was a strict adherence to the worship service outlined in the

---

38. *Ibid.*, 253–55. For an excellent analysis of the meaning of ring shouts, see Lawrence W. Levine, *Black Culture and Black Consciousness* (New York: Oxford University Press, 1977), 38; Payne, *Recollections of Seventy Years*, 255–56.

A.M.E. Discipline. These services were formal and devoid of the spirit which some of the laity thought was necessary when worshiping God. In opposing these people Payne believed he was advancing the cause of racial progress. He saw ring shouts and cornfield ditties as manifestations of ignorance. The fact that these practices may have been of African origin was not important to him for they were not cultural traditions which he wanted black people to maintain. What Payne wanted was to lead his people into the mainstream of American life. An educated ministry, he thought, would accomplish this goal by making their congregations "intelligent and wise."[39]

Theoretically anyone could join the A.M.E. Church. White people could be members but were barred from the clergy. After the Civil War this rule was changed and whites could become ministers in the church. In 1853 a white woman opened a school in Philadelphia for "the education of colored children." Having been ostracized by local whites, she associated largely with the parents who employed her and worshiped at Bethel. After she joined a class some of the black women objected to her presence. Several of them asked Daniel Payne if the laws of the church permitted whites to be members. "I answered that there was no prohibition, and that the A.M.E. Church, like Christianity, ought to be open to all and for all."[40]

The black women of the church were not satisfied with this answer and insisted that she be turned out. Payne visited the pastor of the church, "and finding out that he had authorized the class leader and the local

---

39. Tanner, *Reprint of the First Edition of the Discipline of the African Methodist Episcopal Church*—see the instructions for worship on 56–57. See also, *The Pocket Hymn Book Selected from Different Authors* (Philadelphia: J. H. Cunningham Publishers, 1818). The hymns in this book are similar to those in the standard Methodist hymnal. Together, the *Discipline* and hymnal show how deeply the A.M.E. Church was influenced by European Protestantism. Payne's ascendancy in the church suggests that a new generation of ministers was emerging in the hierarchy. These men were educated and favored more refined church services. Payne was their spokesman. His ideas about the need for an educated clergy are set forth in Charles Killian (ed.), *Sermons and Addresses, 1853–1891* (reprinted New York: Arno Press and New York *Times*, 1972), 7–18, 195–96. See also Henry M. Turner's letter on preaching styles to the *Christian Recorder*, February 20, 1873. This letter indicates Payne was not alone in his opposition to ministerial histrionics.
40. Edward W. Lampton, *Digest of Rulings and Decisions of the A.M.E. Church from 1847–1907* (Washington: Record Publishing Co., 1907), 45–50. Lampton notes that there was some opposition to changing this rule. Payne, *Recollections of Seventy Years*, 115.

preacher to receive her," Payne asked the pastor to defend the woman's rights. He promised to, but did not. Opposition to the woman increased, and she was insulted in and out of class. When this proved insufficient, the women threatened to withhold support from the pastor and starve Payne out, if he continued to maintain the white woman's rights. The pastor gave into their threats and expelled her. In retaliation, Payne refused to give the man a charge at the next conference.[41]

In 1836, 1844, and 1848 anti-Masonic resolutions were introduced at General Conferences of the A.M.E. Church. The 1836 resolution read: "That no preacher be allowed to graduate into ministerial functions who is and continues to be a member of any Freemason lodge." This resolution must not have passed, for in 1844 two petitions against Masonry were presented to the General Conference. These petitions came from Philadelphia and were tabled. The conference ruled since the petitioners "did not specify the evils complained of in their prayers for the suppression of Free Masonry, etc. from the ministry of our church," no action should be taken. In 1848 the issue of Masonry was raised again at a General Conference and was tabled.[42]

Why Masonry became an issue in the church is difficult to say, especially since Richard Allen, the founder, was instrumental in organizing the all-black Prince Hall Lodge in the 1790s. These attempts to prevent A.M.E. ministers from becoming Masons may have been part of a program to control the clergy which developed in the 1840s. In 1840 the General Conference passed a resolution which declared that "[no] travelling preacher is permitted to write or publish any book or pamphlet without the approbation of the annual conference to which he belongs or a committee chosen by them." Before and throughout the 1840s, a number of A.M.E. congregations were torn by power struggles between pastors and boards of trustees over who was to be supreme in church affairs. Another issue which agitated the church in the 1840s was the question of licensing women to preach. In 1844 a resolution calling for the licensing of women preachers was introduced at the General Conference and tabled. Four years later (1848), the General Conference voted to license women preachers. This action was opposed by a minority of delegates led by Daniel Payne. "To license women preachers," they declared, "would introduce

41. Payne, *Recollections of Seventy Years*, 116.
42. Quoted in Arnett, *The Budget*, 168.

distractions into the annual conferences. . . . Such a course as this, is calculated to break up the sacred relations which women bear to their husbands and children, by sending them forth as itinerant preachers, wandering from place to place, to the utter neglect of their household duties and obligations. . . . Such a course is unwarranted by the word of God, and . . . the whole history of the church does not furnish a single instance where the legislative body of a church has ever licensed women to preach." They concluded by describing the measure as "antiscriptural, anti-domestic, and revolutionary." This statement appears to have caused some of the delegates to change their minds and votes. Although in 1852 the issue of women preachers was raised again at the General Conference, it would soon be eclipsed by the problem of slavery.[43]

While other denominations quibbled about slavery and admitted slaveholders as members, the A.M.E. Church excluded them. The New England Conference of the church labeled slavery "a gross outrage against humanity, a positive violation of the Ten Commandments, destructive of all political, moral and religious rites, which is in itself theft, murder, robbery, licentiousness, concubinage, and everything else that is sinful and devilish between heaven and earth." The church could not enter the South; therefore, it condemned slavery in resolutions passed at its conferences.[44]

43. Quoted in Tanner, *An Outline of Our History*, 34–35. Wesley, *Richard Allen*, 93–94; Quoted in Tanner, *An Outline of Our History*, 185; Payne, *History of the African Methodist Episcopal Church*, 223; Tanner, *An Outline of Our History*, 185; *Proceedings of the Eighth General Conference of the A.M.E. Church Held in the City of Philadelphia May 1st, 1848* (Pittsburgh: Berry F. Patterson Printer, 1848), 30. The role which women were to play in the church was an issue that had plagued the church before its founding. In 1803 Dorothy Ripley, an English woman visiting in Philadelphia, asked Allen if she could address the congregation. He refused on the grounds that it was against the rules and Discipline of the Methodist Episcopal Church. For the details of this encounter, see "Some Letters of Richard Allen and Absalom Jones to Dorothy Ripley," *Journal of Negro History*, I (October, 1916), 436–43. After Bethel became independent of the white Methodists, Allen allowed a black woman to preach to the congregation. His change of attitude may be explained, in part, by the fact that he didn't want to antagonize his white superiors in 1803, or Allen may have changed his mind about the role of women in the church, because they did participate in a number of its activities. The woman who requested to be allowed to preach was Jarena Lee, the widow of an A.M.E. minister. Although Allen favored Mrs. Lee's work, a number of his associates did not. For the facts of her career, see Jarena Lee, *The Life and Religious Experience of Jarena Lee, Colored Lady, Giving an Account of Her Call to Preach the Gospel* (Philadelphia: n.p., 1836).
44. Quoted in George A. Singleton, *The Romance of African Methodism* (New York: Exposition Press, 1952), 59; Payne, *History of the African Methodist Episcopal Church*, 328–45.

Along with these resolutions, A.M.E. ministers were instructed to warn their congregations "against a slovenly and ragged appearance, which some . . . are not careful to avoid. . . . Nothing . . . does more to perpetuate the prevailing aversion and prejudice against color. The malignity of prejudice, we believe would be much abated if our people were more careful in their persons and dress, to appear neat and cleanly." The passage of antislavery resolutions and presentation of a respectable black image constitute the twin contributions of the A.M.E. Church to the prewar moral reform movement. Prohibited from entering the South, the church's options were limited. Even if the church had been allowed into the South, the hostility which southerners showed toward northern whites suggests the reception it would have received. The major concern of the A.M.E. Church before the Civil War was setting a moral example, not political and social agitation.[45]

Daniel A. Payne, as one of the church's bishops during the Civil War and Reconstruction, wrote that the creation of the A.M.E. Church "has thrown us upon our own resources and made us tax our own mental powers both for government and support. . . . When we were under the control of the M.E. Church, we were dependent upon them for our ministerial instructions." This made the black man a mere "hearer," a "cipher" in the white church. "The tendency of all this was to prove that the colored man was incapable of self-government and self-support and thereby confirm the oft repeated assertions of his enemies, that he really is incapable of self-government and self-support." The existence of the A.M.E. Church, Payne continued, was a "flat contradiction and triumphant refutation of this slander." For those black men in America who were concerned with uplifting their race, the A.M.E. Church pointed the way.[46]

During the course of the nineteenth century some of the most prominent black men in America would join the church. These included Martin R. Delaney, doctor, explorer, and black nationalist; Henry M. Turner, bishop of the A.M.E. Church, Georgia politician, and African emigrationist; James Lynch, clergyman and Mississippi politician; and Hiram

45. Quoted in Daniel Alexander Payne (ed.), *The Semi-Centenary and the Retrospection of the A.M.E. Church in the United States of America* (Baltimore: Sherwood & Co., 1866), 36.
46. Payne, *History of the African Methodist Episcopal Church*, 9.

Revels, clergyman and senator from Mississippi. All of them joined the church because it was run by blacks and dedicated to improving black peoples' lives.

Although the church which Richard Allen founded encouraged its members to improve themselves, it would be a mistake to assume that these black people were merely emulating their fellow countrymen. If the ideology of pre–Civil War America was individual achievement, as some historians have suggested, the hierarchs and laity of the A.M.E. Church subscribed to this belief system in only a limited way. They may have used the rhetoric of industry and thrift, and urged their people to acquire property, but the intent of these injunctions was different from those of whites.[47]

Individual black men improving themselves did nothing to aid the race as a whole. This point was made by the Reverend Lewis Woodson in his "Ten Letters by Augustine: Moral Work for Colored Men," which appeared in the *Colored American* in 1837 and 1841. Using the pseudonym Augustine, Woodson wrote:

> The general character of any nation or class of men, is determined by the private character of a majority of the individuals who compose it. A few individuals of any class of man, being civilized, enlightened and refined, does not procure for their class such a character. This is the case with Ireland, Spain, Turkey and Russia. Not but that may be found in all these countries many who excel in whatever is elegant, polite and refined; but because a majority of their population are low, ignorant and degraded, it establishes for them a corresponding national character. So on the contrary; France is characterized for her politeness; Scotland for her morality and attention to the duties of religion; Germany for her gravity and profound learning; England for her true greatness and national pride. Not but that there may be found in all of these nations many individuals differing essentially from these national characteristics; but because a majority of the individuals who compose them, are such, it establishes for the whole, such a national character.
>
> So it is, and so it will continue to be with regard to the colored population of the U. States. A majority of them are now in a most

---

47. Lee Benson, *The Concept of Jacksonian Democracy* (Princeton: Princeton University Press, 1961), Ch. 5; Eric Foner, *Free Soil, Free Labor, Free Men* (New York: Oxford University Press, 1970), Ch. 1; Rush Welter, *The Mind of America, 1820–1860* (New York: Columbia University Press, 1975), Ch. 7.

degraded condition; and this has stamped the character of degradation upon the whole race. The few who have risen above the condition of the many, are not regarded; nor need they expect to be.
Their virtues and attainments will never be fully appreciated, until
the majority of the class with whom they are identified, have risen
to something like a level with themselves. Hence, the necessity of
making an adequate effort for *general* moral improvement.

The improvement which Allen, Woodson, and the other black leaders
called for could only be achieved in a limited way. What they did not understand was the ideological function which their peoples' degradation
served in American society.[48]

In a country where status was earned rather than ascribed, blacks occupied the lowest rung on the social ladder. White men moving up in this
world could always look back (or down) and see what awaited them if
they failed. Fearing failure, they continued to strive and at the same time
excluded most Negroes from the arena of competition. Those blacks who
did succeed found themselves classed with their less fortunate brothers.
In brief, nineteenth-century blacks were damned if they did succeed and
damned if they did not. Finally, the later experiences of Allen's followers
during the Civil War and Reconstruction eras show that many of the
problems discussed above continued to plague the church.

48. Sterling Stuckey (ed.), *The Ideological Origins of Black Nationalism* (Boston: Beacon
Press, 1972), 121. For details of Woodson's life, see Floyd J. Miller, "The Father of
Black Nationalism: Another Contender," *Civil War History*, XVII (December, 1971),
310–20. For an explication of these anxieties, see Leonard L. Richards, *Gentlemen of
Property and Standing* (New York: Oxford University Press, 1970). For a case study of
nineteenth-century Negro decline, see Theodore Hershberg, "Free Blacks in Antebellum
Philadelphia: A Study of Ex-Slaves, Freeborn, and Socio Economic Decline," *Journal of
Social History*, V (Winter, 1971), 183–209. See also Frank J. Webb's delightful novel,
The Garies and Their Friends (1857; reprinted New York: Arno Press and New York
Times*, 1969).

II A Millennium of Peace and Hope

"The Civil War," Robert Penn Warren has observed, "is for the American imagination the great single event of our history." But from the day that Fort Sumter was fired on, northern whites and Negroes perceived the war in very different ways. Most northern white people thought that the war was being fought to preserve the union, and not to free the slaves, and even after abolition became an aim of the war, they did not envision that it would make Negroes their equals. For Negroes and their abolitionist allies the war represented an enactment of Old and New Testament prophecies which foretold the coming of a millennium.[1]

During the course of their sojourn in America, Negroes had come to think of their experience as similar to that of the Jews in Egypt. They were an oppressed people whom God in the fullness of time would de-

1. Robert Penn Warren, *The Legacy of the Civil War* (New York: Random House, 1961), 3. See also James McPherson, *The Struggle for Equality* (Princeton: Princeton University Press, 1964); August Meier, "Negroes in the First and Second Reconstruction of the South," *Civil War History*, XIII (June, 1967), 114–31. For a masterful explication of northern attitudes on the eve of the Civil War, see Foner, *Free Soil, Free Labor, Free Men*. Northern ambivalence about the purpose of the war is explored in James B. Stewart, *Holy Warriors* (New York: Hill and Wang, 1976); and Forrest G. Wood, *The Black Scare* (Berkeley and Los Angeles: University of California Press, 1968); Ira Brown, "Watchers for the Second Coming: The Millenarian Tradition in America," *Mississippi Valley Historical Review*, XXIX (1952–53), 441–58; and Ernest Lee Tuveson: *Redeemer Nation: The Idea of America's Millenial Role* (Chicago: University of Chicago Press, 1968). This book contains some interesting material on America's millenial expectations of the Civil War in Chapter 6. The millenial expectations of black people in America have not been examined in depth, but for a good beginning see Levine, *Black Culture and Black Consciousness*, Ch. 1 and Leon F. Litwack, "Free at Last," in Tamara K. Hareven (ed.), *Anonymous Americans: Exploration in Nineteenth Century Social History* (Englewood Cliffs: Prentice-Hall, 1971), 131–71.

liver from bondage. The Civil War was God's vehicle of deliverance. Internecine strife, they believed, would purge the nation of the sin of slavery and eradicate those barriers which had prevented them from entering the mainstream of American life. While the battle raged, the Negro could not be idle. It was important that he participate in the war of liberation. A study of the position of the African Methodist Episcopal Church on the question of black participation in the war effort reveals shifts in the church's overall response to the Civil War. These shifts can be identified by examining the ways in which the church addressed these questions. First, how did the church perceive the war? Second, how did it define the black man's role in the conflict? Finally, once the war was concluded and peace was restored, how did the hierarchy and members of the A.M.E. Church conceive of their role in a reunited nation?[2]

1   President Lincoln's call for troops in April of 1861 evoked a positive response among some northern free blacks. Shortly after his call for volunteers, groups of black men in Boston, New York, and Philadelphia met and decided to organize militia units. These men believed that if they demonstrated their patriotism, manhood, and courage on the battlefield, the nation would be morally obligated to grant them citizenship and equal rights. After the outbreak of the war, Frederick Douglass was the most outspoken proponent of black enlistment and argued for it in the following ways. Manhood, Douglass asserted, required the black man to take sides; he was "either for the Government or against the Government." He was a citizen as well as a man, and citizenship brought with it the obligation of serving one's country when it was in peril. Every Negro hater and lover of slavery, moreover, viewed the arming of Negroes as a calamity. The Negro should learn the use of arms, Douglass advised, for "the only way open to any race to make their rights respected is to learn how to defend them." By enlisting, the Negro would demonstrate his courage and disprove the slanders against his people, establish his right of citizenship in the country, and recover his self-respect. Finally, enlistment would be "one of the most certain means of preventing the country

---

2.   The A.M.E. belief that the Civil War was a war of deliverance was shared by President Lincoln. See William J. Wolf, *The Religion of Abraham Lincoln* (New York: The Seabury Press, 1963), 24.

from drifting back into the whirlpool of pro-slavery compromise at the end of the war." Whatever men decided to call it, Douglass declared, "the war for the Union," was "a war for Emancipation."[3]

At the outset, however, Douglass' optimism and his belief in the importance of Negro participation in the war were shared neither by the hierarchy nor by most members of the A.M.E. Church. In an editorial of April 20, 1861, the church's newspaper, the *Christian Recorder*, took a view of the war that differed sharply from that of Douglass. "What is the cause of all this tumult?" the newspaper asked. "Is it really the Negro?" The answer was "No!" "We wish here to correct a very great error in the minds of many of our white friends with regard to the relation of colored people and the war; that is they are fighting about negroes. This is not true." The war was being waged over the territories, but not over whether Negroes or whites should occupy them. The quarrel, said the *Christian Recorder*, was between North and South, both trying to prevent each other from occupying the western territories. Any perusal of the various daily papers, the editorial contended, would show that the South was defending its constitutional rights.[4]

To the *Christian Recorder*, it was essentially a political struggle between two political parties. The Democrats did not want to submit to the control of the Republicans, and the Republicans, having submitted for a number of years to Democratic rule, thought they should be "allowed to shape the policy of the Government according to their ideas." Not the Negro question, but disagreements over who was to settle the territories and govern the country had led to war. Since the Negro was merely an observer in this national crisis, and not a participant in it, what was he to do? The *Recorder* advised its readers to pray to "Almighty God, for his mercy and holy wisdom." Prayer would restore peace to the strife-torn country.

When peace was not immediately restored, the A.M.E. Church again expressed its opposition to Douglass by advising black men not to enlist

3. McPherson, *The Struggle for Equality*, 192. For Douglass' ideas about the war, see Philip S. Foner (ed.), *The Life and Writing of Frederick Douglass* (New York: International Publishers, 1952), III, 32.
4. *Christian Recorder*, April 20, 1861. For another opinion about the causes of the war, see *Christian Recorder* for November 30, 1861. In a letter to the paper H. M. Turner wrote that "every person knows that the national strife now agitating this country is about the thraldomized condition of the colored man." Later on this opinion would become the official one of the church.

in the Union army. This advice was based on a historical analysis of the Negroes' position in American society. In both the Revolution and the War of 1812, the *Christian Recorder* noted, blacks had fought for this country. "But now that treason arms itself to overthrow a constitutional Government, where will they be? What is their duty in 1861?" Although some black men, like Douglass, were urging other blacks to enlist, the *Christian Recorder* dissented, stating that the American Negro had no reason to fight for a country which had always oppressed him, and which had been oppressing him ever more severely since 1800. In most northern states, on the eve of the Civil War, free Negroes were a proscribed people, politically, socially, and economically. This process had begun before the War of 1812, and by 1860 Negroes were systematically separated from whites in most facets of life. Negroes were either excluded from public transportation or forced to sit in "Jim Crow" sections, and similar conditions also obtained in lecture halls and theaters, where blacks sat, when permitted, in galleries or secluded corners. Resorts, hotels, and restaurants barred Negroes unless they were servants accompanying their employers. Proscriptions also extended to the realms of political and civil rights. Although most northern states barred Negroes from the polls and prohibited them from serving on juries, discrimination did not end at the polls and jury box. In a society which boasted of expanding opportunity and social mobility, Negro laborers struggled daily to earn enough to keep themselves and their families alive. Hostile native and immigrant white workers and bigoted trade unions forced those blacks who were able to find employment into unskilled and low-paying jobs. In short, the black man in pre–Civil War northern society was at best a "denizen." He was neither an "alien" nor a "citizen" and possessed, according to Chief Justice Roger Taney of the Supreme Court, "no rights which the white man was bound to respect."[5]

Cognizant of their people's disadvantaged position in American society, the hierarchy of the A.M.E. Church urged black men not to enlist in the Union army. "Before the formation of the American Union, our citizenship was a fact acknowledged and respected. Hence our right to fight in defense of our country was undisputed." But after the "American Gov-

---

5. Quoted in Stanley S. Kutler (ed.), *The Dred Scott Decision* (Boston: Houghton Mifflin Company, 1967), 13. For a discussion of the concept of "denizenship," see Litwack, *North of Slavery*, 53.

ernment commenced its career of glory," the position of Negroes had
gradually changed: "Until now in 1861, not only our citizenship, but ev-
en our common humanity is denied. Denied alike in the sanctuary of the
most High, as it is on the floors of the state and national Legislatures. The
same cruel prejudice which excludes us from the halls of science also re-
pels us from the militia and standing army. Therefore to offer ourselves
for military service now, is to abandon self-respect, and invite insult
. . . [and] those who so acted manifest, indeed, Commendable Zeal, at
the same time that they betray that modest prudence which should always characterize a conscious manhood." Before black men signed up,
the hierarchs decreed, the government would have to grant them political
and civil rights.[6]

In adopting this stance, the church was criticizing and rebuking Douglass and those other blacks who enthusiastically had endorsed the Union
cause. A "conscious manhood," the churchmen believed, required that
blacks be skeptical about the war. When President Lincoln designated the
last Thursday in September, 1861, as "a day of humiliation, prayer, and
fasting for all the people of the nation," Jabez P. Campbell, the eighth
bishop of the church, articulated this skepticism. "Did the President, in
all of this proclamation, or in any part of it, mean and intend to include
the colored people?" The answer was no. "The President is not now and
never was either an abolitionist or anti-slavery man." There was no quarrel between the president and the South on the slavery question. "He, his
Cabinet, and all of his official organs most steadily proclaim that this is
not a war against slavery, but a war for the Union, to save slavery in the
Union. The President intends that the Union shall be preserved as it was,
when he came into power, the chief cornerstone of which was slavery."
The president, moreover, conceived of the Constitution as "an instrument
of compromise between slavery and freedom" and subscribed to the Dred
Scott Decision, which held that "black men have no rights that white men
are bound to respect." Little wonder, then, Bishop Campbell charged,
that President Lincoln should have interfered with the work of Generals
Butler and Frémont and returned confiscated slaves to their owners.

To Bishop Campbell, the truly perfidious nature of the Lincoln administration could be seen even more explicitly in its refusal to accept black
enlistments in the Union army. "By all these acts," he concluded, "the

6. *Christian Recorder*, April 27, 1861.

President means to show to the nation, both Union men and rebels, that he does not recognize black men, neither expressly nor impliedly to be part and parcel of this nation." Bishop Campbell's accusations were more than an exercise in clerical pique or bombast; they pointed to the administration's dilatory handling of the problems of emancipation and Negro enlistment. The president knew that a large segment of the northern white populace opposed emancipation of the slaves and the use of black troops in the Union war effort. Any action on these issues would be seen as an abolitionist plot to grant the Negro equal rights and citizenship. Fearful of alienating white workers in the North and Northeast, settlers in the Midwest, and Unionists in the border states, the president remained silent on these issues for the first year and a half of the war. Public opinion and military necessity ultimately forced him to act on these problems.[7]

2   As the war dragged on, the church's attitude entered a new phase which was related in part to a new sensibility towards emancipation on the part of northern whites. For over thirty years the abolitionists had warned the people of the Free States that slavery was destroying the nation. By and large they had been either ignored or denounced as fanatics, but with the outbreak of hostilities northerners began to view the abolitionists in a new light. No longer regarded as zealots or crackpots, they were seen as prophets who had tried to save their country before it was too late. The new esteem which the abolitionists basked in, however, did not extend to the people they championed. Popular acceptance of the idea of emancipation did not modify northern attitudes toward the Negro, who was still feared and hated by the majority of northern whites. Northern whites wanted to free the slaves as a "military necessity" to preserve the Union but did not want to grant the freedmen equal rights and citizenship.[8]

7. *Christian Recorder*, October 12, 1861; see also "The National Fast and the Negro," for another critique of Union war policy and appeasement of the rebels. A discussion of the Negroes' participation in the war may be found in Dudley Taylor Cornish, *The Sable Arm* (New York: W. W. Norton & Co., 1966). McPherson traces the changes in northern public opinion on the question of Negro enlistment in Chapter 9 of *The Struggle for Equality*. See also Wood, *The Black Scare*, 40–41. Chapter 2 of *The Black Scare* contains an interesting discussion of northern fears of emancipation. For an examination of border state opposition to emancipation, see Charles L. Wagandt, *The Mighty Revolution: Negro Emancipation in Maryland, 1862–1864* (Baltimore: The Johns Hopkins University Press, 1964).
8. McPherson, *The Struggle for Equality*, 82; James G. Randall and David Donald, *The Civil War and Reconstruction* (2nd ed.; Boston: D. C. Heath and Co., 1961), 373–75;

These attitudes were reflected in President Lincoln's initial proposals for compensated emancipation and colonization. In November of 1861 Lincoln drafted two bills for compensated emancipation in Delaware, proposing that the government finance the project by selling $700,000 worth of 6 percent bonds, which would pay for the proposal in five years. This suggestion and others like it were circulated in the Delaware legislature, but they met with strong opposition and were ultimately voted down. Before their defeat, when Lincoln was optimistic about their enactment in Delaware, the president asked Congress in his annual message in 1861 to consider the possibility and pass legislation providing for compensation and colonization. Convinced that free Negroes would never be accepted as equals by white Americans, the president sent to Congress in March of 1862 a special message on the question of compensated emancipation. This message was severely criticized by Henry M. Turner, a prominent A.M.E. minister. He cautioned Negroes not to believe that the emancipation proposal portended "hope for a brighter day." The document, he said, was an "ingenious subterfuge." Turner then pinpointed a major flaw in Lincoln's proposal: "After recommending [emancipation], it denies that Congress has any power to legislate on slavery [and] leaves it under the absolute control of individual states." Turner also suggested that blacks consider the implications of the proposal to give financial aid which states might use in any way they chose. "In that phrase," Turner observed, "there is a broad field, a wide space, an ocean of thought." The president's emancipation plan rested on the assumption that liberated slaves could not remain in the United States. He did not wish to increase the free Negro population and thus frighten northern whites, who feared that after emancipation their states would be flooded with blacks and subsequently Africanized. Compensated emancipation and colonization, Lincoln believed, would rid the country of a troublesome people.[9]

On August 14, 1862, Lincoln met with some free Negroes. He informed them that the government was going to make funds available for the colonization of persons of African descent. It was his intention, he told the blacks, to pursue such a policy. Racial differences, Lincoln said, divided the races and operated to the disadvantage of both groups. Indeed, white

John Hope Franklin, *The Emancipation Proclamation* (New York: Doubleday & Co., 1963), 22–23.
9. *Christian Recorder*, March 22, 1862; Wood, *The Black Scare*, Ch. 2.

men were not fighting and killing one another because of the Negro. American Negroes, Lincoln continued, should be willing to go to another land to help people who were not as fortunate as themselves. Lincoln's interview received wide coverage in the press and was read by many blacks.[10]

The pros and cons of colonization had been debated in the black community for more than forty years. During this time the A.M.E. Church had opposed various schemes aimed at removing the Negro from America. Although the church agreed with the president "that there [were] strong prejudices in the minds of probably a plurality of white men," they felt that officials who were "appointed and elected to execute the laws of any country" should not "succumb" to popular prejudices. "The colored people have been tillers of the soil and supporters of this government, and in every sense of the word born [sic] a part of the burden and beat of this country." Hence the A.M.E. Church opposed Lincoln's colonization proposal. They believed it was part of an unscrupulous plan to send the Negroes away just as freedom was dawning for them. "It would appear to all intelligent minds in this country, as well as other countries, that so long as white men could keep the people of color under the scale of ignorance and oppression, it was all right, and that this was the country for the blacks." Throughout the war the A.M.E. Church would continue to oppose plans to colonize blacks outside the United States, because they believed that Negroes were Americans and should not be removed from their homeland. In time, this sense of Americanism would also alter the church's attitude toward the war.[11]

By March of 1862 the church discerned that the "moral sentiment of the people" in the North was changing. More northerners were demanding "that the wicked system of human bondage" be ended. They were now saying that the war, which was "distracting the land from one end to the other," had grown out of the conflict between slavery and the moral principles of the North. The A.M.E. Church welcomed this development but found the new white view naive. The church insisted that black men had to participate in the quest for freedom, because there never would be "any peace in this country until the black men [had] a hand and a say-so

10. For a description of this meeting see Benjamin Quarles, *Lincoln and the Negro* (New York: Oxford University Press, 1962), 108.
11. *Christian Recorder*, August 23, 1862; For another criticism of the Proclamation see October 4, 1862.

in the bringing about of peace." Northerners were naive to believe that an accursed institution such as slavery could be abolished peacefully. Slavery was an evil which had "plundered cradles, separated husbands and wives, parents and children." It had "starved to death, worked to death, whipped to death, run to death, burned to death, lied to death, kicked and cuffed to death" generations of blacks. "Worst of all," it had "made prostitutes of a majority of the best women of a whole nation of people, against their will." It was stupid to think that such a monster would die easily and "no one but the most stupid jackass . . . could be guilty of supposing such a thing." The war would not end until the Negro was allowed to fight. It was "God's design" that both white and colored men put down the rebellion.[12]

In July of 1862, the church's desire to have Negroes serve in the Union army received a boost when Congress passed a bill empowering the president to "employ as many of the colored people as he thinks necessary." Congress' action was both "good" and "right," the *Christian Recorder* observed, but it was not enough. To fight for the Union, Negroes had to have "all the rights accorded to other human beings in the United States." Throughout the first year and a half of the war the government had dodged the issue of Negro enlistment and civil rights. Within the A.M.E. Church, the Lincoln administration's timidity on these questions had been viewed as foolhardy and dangerous. God was punishing the North because of its intransigence. He was raining down plagues on the Union army. The riots in Baltimore, the defeat at Bull Run, the death of General Lyon, and the *Merrimac*'s destruction of the Union fleet at Norfolk were manifestations of God's displeasure. God would send even more horrendous plagues if the Union did not rectify its ways.[13]

The A.M.E. Church now began to stress the importance of unity and advised northerners to look at the enemy and learn something. Whether they were black or white men, the rebels were united. "They used all the means in their power to conquer whom they considered their foes." The Union, by contrast, was divided over the Negro. There was no excuse for such divisiveness. Negroes were "able-bodied, reared on American soil, and have ever proved themselves loyal to the same." They had an even better claim to the rights of American citizenship than any newly arrived

12. *Christian Recorder*, March 29, 1862; July 19, 1862; July 30, 1864.
13. *Christian Recorder*, July 19, 1862; July 12, 1862.

foreigner. Their forefathers had helped to secure American independence, spilling the first blood in that struggle.[14]

The church's call for unity did not, however, stifle persistent criticism of the government's hypocrisy, which prompted one *Christian Recorder* correspondent to advise blacks to stay in their own states and let the whites kill one another. "Ought it not to be the true policy of this Government," he asked, "to wipe away unjustifiable prejudice which has been shown to exist against what God has seen fit to make for his own Glory the black and white races?" God had "made a variety of species, kind, and color," in "his infinite power and wisdom." And yet, he charged, in the face of God's wisdom, the War Department, "and about ⅓ of the Union men" say they "will not do this or that, if the colored people . . . are to be formed into regiments or brigades." If Negroes joined the army, some disgruntled Americans threatened to throw down their arms or refuse to enlist. While these Union men, "as they call themselves, are standing still and harping on nothing, the Rebel Confederacy, officers, privates and subjects seem to be a unit irrespective of color or grade, and use every means in their power to destroy the Union men at all points, asking or giving no quarter."[15]

Lincoln's Emancipation Proclamation seemed to turn the war against slavery and it made enlistment in the army more popular among black leaders. The issue, however, remained a divisive one in the A.M.E. Church. This time the ambivalence stemmed from clear evidence of racial discrimination in the Union army. Black soldiers were paid less than white troops and were not given the clothing allowance granted their cohorts. "Will they fight?" "Should they fight?" These two questions were debated in the church after the call for "colored soldiers" in February of 1863. In response to the first question the answer was yes. The Negro would fight if it was necessary. There had never been a period in the world's history where Negroes had "failed to show their courage." The basically affirmative answer to the second question was hedged with qualifications. At the same time black men were warned to exercise some discretion and not "take any hasty steps." Before enlisting they should know "whether they [were] to have all the rights and privileges of other citizens in every state of the Union, and as any other soldier according to their rank." The ques-

14. *Christian Recorder*, August 9, 1862.
15. *Christian Recorder*, August 16, 1862.

tion of equal rights in the Union army was extremely important to members of the church. Letters written to the *Christian Recorder* during 1863/64 stressed this concern. Equality meant equal pay, protection, and advancement. "If the Government wants black men to fight as well as white, why not pay them as good wages? Do they wish them to fight less than white men? Or do they suppose that a rebel killed by a black man will not be as dead, and incapable of doing mischief, as one killed by an Irishman, or a German." [16]

The savage treatment that black troops received when captured by Confederate soldiers provided church members with still another issue. Why should black men leave their homes and jobs and be "sent to South Carolina, or Georgia to fight rebel white men, with the prospects of a dog's death [at the hands of] the minions of Jeff Davis." What they wanted from the government was the recognition of their "manhood as soldiers, the same wages, the same protection as others." If they were captured in battle and hung by the Confederates, the government should "demand a white rebel's head for every loyal colored man hung by the secessionist." [17]

Members of the church were also angered by the army's discriminatory promotional policies. "If the country requires the aid of our strong armed men," one member wrote, "those seeking them must give place and preferment, to men of character, worth and influence, among colored people." In most regiments, he continued, Negroes were outranked by white men who were their inferiors. These whites held their positions solely because of their color. "Give us," he concluded, "from among the colored people, chaplains, officers, matrons, nurses, teachers, recruiters, contractors, traders, surgeons, if you would have our hearty cooperation." [18]

Several months after the president's proclamation, the annual conference of the A.M.E. Church passed a resolution calling for black people to support the Negro troops. "[I]t is the duty of the entire colored people of the North, to throw their arms and influence around these truly patriotic men, and inspire them with the most exalted devotion to the Cause, in which they have enlisted." Just why the church changed its position on black enlistment is not clear. Whatever the reason, the door was now open

16. McPherson, *The Struggle for Equality*, 212; *Christian Recorder*, February 14, 1863; March 12, 1864; February 14, 1863.
17. *Christian Recorder*, February 14, 1863.
18. *Christian Recorder*, January 9, 1864.

for the members and clergy of the A.M.E. Church to enlist in the Union army. Among the first to do so was Henry M. Turner.[19]

On September 10, 1863, Turner was inducted into the United States Army and commissioned as chaplain of the First United States Colored Regiment. He was the first man of color to receive such a commission. As a chaplain, Turner would urge other black men to enlist. He had been a persistent critic of the government's policies and his criticisms did not end after he entered service. Unlike some black leaders, however, Turner was not disturbed by the fact that Congress had barred black officers from commanding white troops. He thought this was "one of the best features" of the enlistment bill. "I still hope that it will be so arranged, that no brigade, corps, or command will be permitted to intermit." If black and white troops were to serve together, Turner feared, racial clashes would break out. Inevitably, "some prejudicial sap-head soldier will be apt to endeavor to throw some contumelious epithets at the nigger as the Irishman says." To avoid such situations Turner proposed that the troops be separated, a suggestion consistent with the A.M.E. philosophy of ex-emplification. If blacks and whites served together, "whatever honor we might be entitled to, would be conferred upon someone else, and the Ne-gro set down as coward." It was important, then, for black people to have their own soldiers and officers in separate units. "Then bid us strike for our liberty, and if we deserve any merit it will stand out beyond contra-dictions, and if we deserve none . . . then brand us with the stigmatic in-famy of cowardly dupes."[20]

In going to war and supporting the Union, A.M.E. Church members shared the sentiments and aspirations of most northern blacks, who be-lieved that "slavery had been a war upon the Negro race for two hundred years." By enlisting in the Union cause, black people were dramatizing their demand for "equal pay, equal bounty, equal pensions, equal rights, equal privileges, and equal suffrage to all citizens." Their ultimate aim was the "reconstruction" of the South through the abolition of slavery and the establishment of republican forms of government.[21]

19. *Christian Recorder*, May 23, 1863.
20. *Christian Recorder*, February 14, 1863. Turner's example was followed by two other ministers of the church, William Hunter and T. G. Stewart.
21. *Christian Recorder*, June 27, 1863.

In calling for black troops the nation had at least realized that its salvation was not in its own hands. That was the way the A.M.E. Church tended to view it. The people of the North had learned that liberty was the birthright of all the sons of Adam. "Who can tell but in the economy of God the long years of suffering endured by the African race shall not eventuate in the salvation, as well as the punishment of Anglo Americans!" The Negro as saviour was a theme constantly reiterated by church members. "I do most certainly believe," wrote one of them, "the colored people of this country are destined to be the people that will save this nation from God's fiery indignation because of [its] political sins."[22]

"Among the nations of the earth, the United States," like others, had "sinned against God." For more than two hundred years the country had sinned until its "sins reached up to heaven." The war was God's punishment. His instrument of justice was war, "and we shall never have permanent peace again until our national sins have all purged away." In purging the land God intended to "deliver the spoils out of the hands of the spoiler and the oppressed out of oppression." To expiate this sin it was important that the Negro serve in the Union army, a condition that required a change of attitudes in the North. During the first year and a half of the conflict, white northerners had been deceived. Believing that the war was a white man's war, they had refused the Negroes' offer of help. Though blacks had tried to dissuade whites from this position, their advice had not been heeded. Hence blacks had decided to "stand still and see the salvation of God, and let the white man go out and try it alone, so that they might become painfully convinced that this was not altogether the white man's war, but the negroes' also." But the whites had failed, and the reasons were apparent to the church. God had ordained a mission for America which in no way envisioned the segregation of the races. Such a separation ran counter to the divine plan that this continent should "be the great field of training for the development of [the] human mind, the display of genius, and solving the great problem of a universal brotherhood, the unity of the race of mankind, and the eternal principles of intellectual, moral, and spiritual development."[23]

What these black people were saying was that, unlike their white brothers, they recognized in the stability of the United States Government a

22. *Christian Recorder*, February 14, 1863.
23. *Christian Recorder*, October 8, 1864; February 27, 1864; February 14, 1863.

source of strength to other nations. While this government stood, "there [was] hope for the most abject, disabled and helpless of mankind." This belief had sustained them through their sojourn in America. Once the rebellion was subdued there would be a "millennium of peace." The nation would come "out of the ordeal regenerated and purified of enemies open and enemies covert." Never before had conditions in the country looked brighter. A glorious future awaited Americans "with the nation saved and the Negro redeemed to prove his manhood both on this continent and in his fatherland."[24]

3   The rhetoric that A.M.E. Church members used to describe the Civil War and their people's participation in the conflict is misleading: for they did not really believe that the war would completely transform their position in American society. Although they used a language which was rich in biblical imagery, these black folk knew that once the hostilities ceased they would have to struggle on another front. In fighting for the Union the Negro had demonstrated his manhood and shown that he was capable of doing what any other man could do. Once the hostilities ceased, however, the black man would still face difficulties. The new struggle was to be waged against what one A.M.E. minister called "the wrong moral sentiment of the nation." Members of the church realized that the destruction of slavery did not herald a change in the nation's racial attitudes. Most American whites, they knew, still considered black people to be their racial, social, and cultural inferiors. But if the black man was to become an integral part of the Republic, these attitudes and the behavior which they sustained would have to be eradicated. White Americans would have to be shown that black people were their equals. The clergy and members of the A.M.E. Church believed that the best way to accomplish this was for blacks to become respectable property owners.[25]

The program of uplift which the church advocated was not new. Throughout the first half of the nineteenth century black people had been urged by their churches, leading spokesmen, and newspapers to acquire property and educate themselves and their children. In short, by becoming respectable members of the communities in which they lived, they

24. *Christian Recorder*, October 8, 1864; October 1, 1864; July 18, 1863.
25. *Christian Recorder*, October 1, 1864.

"would elevate the race," become independent, and disprove the claims
of white racists that blacks were an inferior and improvident people who
could not survive in a free society. From its founding the A.M.E. Church
had worked to disprove such assumptions. Members of the organization
were urged to become models of probity; their example, it was believed,
would inspire other blacks to do the same. Imbued with the idea that
their mission in America was to elevate the race at home and abroad, the
members of the church saw in the Civil War an opportunity to accelerate
the process of black uplift. With the demise of slavery, they thought, the
principal barrier to black advancement would be removed.[26]

Anticipating a society without slavery, the church had begun urging
black people early in the war to change their ways. On May 4, 1861, an
editorial in the *Christian Recorder* urged Negroes who were not gainfully
employed to leave the cities and seek employment in the countryside. "If
nine-tenths of our people, in a place like Philadelphia where many of
them have nothing to do, would move out [to] the country and learn to
fell trees, split rails, clear forests, and till the ground; raise wheat, corn,
oats, and potatoes, they would soon, and that very soon, find themselves
in an independent position, as far as food and raiment are concerned."
These suggestions presaged a veritable chorus of injunctions to blacks in
general to acquire property, to make money, to become educated, and to
enter useful occupations. The paper continued to make such suggestions
throughout the war. The purpose was to create a self-sufficient Negro
community which would eventually be able to exercise some political
power. To achieve this goal the church urged Negroes to migrate to the
unsettled lands of the West and Southwest and there establish all-black
communities. All that these lands required was the "magic touch of industry," and their wealth would pour forth to enrich the country. The
people occupying these territories would become an important element
in the nation. "It is to be supposed that that element of national strength
which shall by their industry and energy develop the immense resources
of wealth which this vast region of country is capable, and turns the vast
revenue arising therefrom into the treasury of the nation are to be consid-

26. Frederick Cooper, "Elevating the Race: The Social Thought of Black Leaders, 1827–
    1850," 604–26. See also Pease and Pease, *They Who Would Be Free*, 95–141; *Chris-
    tian Recorder*, March 26, 1864 and November 21, 1868; James Lynch, *The Mission of
    the United States Republic* (Augusta, Ga.: Steam Power Press Chronicle & Sentinel Of-
    fice, 1865), 12.

ered any mean portion of the national family." If the Negro did not do this or something like it, he faced a grim future in America. Black people could not depend on charity or the government to look after them once the war was over. No people could expect to be lifted up entirely by the "labors or benevolence of others." As long as black people were pensioners of other people's pity they would be disparaged. But as soon as their dependence was broken and the world knew that Negroes were not mendicants, but men, they would be accepted into the American community.[27]

Recent scholarship suggests that this expectation was unrealistic. The creation of a propertied black community in nineteenth-century America could not have and in fact did not change the country's racial attitudes. Black people were not proscribed because of their lack of property but because of their color and what it connoted in American society. The church's campaign to improve the Negroes' economic position was commendable, but their assumption that such improvement could affect the Negroes' manhood was naive and indicated their abandonment of the skeptical, distrustful attitude toward American society that they had expressed in the early stages of the war. The campaign for improvement represented a total misreading of the times and a misunderstanding of how the destruction of slavery would contribute to the strengthening rather than the diminution of racial prejudice. But believing that God was the prime mover of history and that history itself was progressive, the A.M.E. Church believed once that war was over it could push on successfully, in quest of a millennium of peace and hope.[28]

27. *Christian Recorder*, May 4, 1861; November 30, 1861; May 31, 1862; February 21, 1863; May 23, 1863; April 23, 1864; May 7, 1864; March 25, 1865; August 12, 1865; August 19, 1865; May 19, 1866; April 23, 1864; April 30, 1864.
28. For the evolution of American racial attitudes before 1812, see Winthrop D. Jordan, *White Over Black: American Attitudes Toward the Negro, 1550–1812* (Chapel Hill: University of North Carolina Press, 1968); Fredrickson, *The Black Image in the White Mind*.

III "I Seek My Brethren"

GENESIS XXXVII:16

1   From its beginning in 1863 the A.M.E. Church's mission to the freedmen was deeply influenced by the ideology of the pre–Civil War moral reform movement. The church's mission to the freed bondsman was based on the belief that human nature was perfectible, and that if the social order which oppressed the black man were rearranged, he would become a productive citizen. In the South this meant slavery had to be destroyed because it oppressed both blacks and whites. With slavery's demise, southerners of both colors could create a model society. A.M.E. leaders believed education was the key to this new social order. Their belief in the power of education was naive and the A.M.E. missionaries were soon to learn that it could not bind the country or the races together. To think that it would displayed a faith in man which nineteenth-century black men could ill afford. But, believing that "revolutions do not go backwards," they went South in search of their brethren.[1]

The Negro churches in Washington set aside Sunday, April 3, 1862, as a day of thanksgiving and prayer, hoping that the president would sign the District of Columbia Emancipation Act passed by Congress on April 11 into law. This measure would emancipate the slaves in Washington and compensate loyal masters for their loss of property. At one of these services, Daniel Alexander Payne preached a sermon entitled "Welcome

---

1. For discussions of the pre–Civil War reform movement, see David J. Rothman, *The Discovery of the Asylum* (Boston: Little, Brown, 1971); Alice Felt Tyler, *Freedom's Ferment* (1944; reprinted New York: Harper Torchbook, 1962); Ronald G. Walters, *American Reformers, 1815–1860* (New York: Hill & Wang, 1978); *Christian Recorder*, May 7, 1964.

to the Ransomed." Three days after the sermon was delivered, President Lincoln signed the measure.[2]

Payne's sermon was more than an exercise in Christian courtesy; it welcomed the freedmen and at the same time outlined the "Duties of the Colored Inhabitants of the District of Columbia." Their principal task was to welcome the freedmen to the "churches, homesteads, and social circles" of black Washingtonians. "Enter the great family of Holy Freedom," Payne urged, "not to lounge in sinful indolence, not to degrade yourselves by vice, nor to corrupt society by licentiousness . . . but to the enjoyment of a well regulated liberty." If the ex-slaves were to survive as free men, it was important that they adopt habits of "industry and thrift" and at the same time become religious and law abiding. These virtues would be learned by observing the respectable black people of Washington. The essence of Payne's message was the Protestant ethic: industry, sobriety, thrift, and piety were the keys to success and salvation in America.[3]

Although this oration was intended to help the newly freed slaves of the District of Columbia, it was also aimed at the thousands of contrabands located in camps around the city. Shortly after the war began, Washington became a haven for slaves fleeing from Virginia and Maryland.[4]

In late 1862, President Lincoln made a decision that promised to multiply greatly the number of freedmen—and the problems of the A.M.E. Church. On September 22, Lincoln issued a preliminary emancipation proclamation, warning the slaveholders of the rebellious states that he would declare their slaves free unless they laid down their arms by January 1, 1863. Shortly after the president's announcement, Henry M. Turner issued "A Call to Action" to the members of the A.M.E. Church. The president's announcement, Turner told his fellow churchmen, which in one hundred days would liberate thousands of slaves, "has opened up a new series of obligations, consequences, and results, never known" to our forefathers. These "obligations" were to the contrabands and to their changed "material," "political," and "social condition." The day when Negroes could be "inactive," "disinterested," and "irresponsible," Turner asserted, had passed. A new era demanded "every intellectual fiber" of

2. Benjamin Quarles, *Lincoln and the Negro* (New York: Oxford University Press, 1962), 103; Daniel Alexander Payne, *Welcome to the Ransomed, or Duties of the Colored Inhabitants of the District of Columbia* (Baltimore: Bull & Tuttle, 1862).
3. Payne, *Welcome to the Ransomed*, 6–8.
4. Quarles, *Lincoln and the Negro*, 77; *Christian Recorder*, April 5, 1862.

the black man. The time for "boasting of ancestral genius" and "prowling through the dusty pages of ancient history to find a specimen of Negro intellectuality" was over. It was now time for free black men to turn their attention to the thousands of slave refugees flocking to Union lines. Winter was approaching and the refugees were destitute. Every black man, woman, or child "who [had] a speck of grace or a bit of sympathy" for the race that they were inseparably identified with was called upon by "force of surrounding circumstances to extend a hand of mercy to bone of our bone and flesh of our flesh."[5]

In the wake of Turner's appeal, the congregations of the A.M.E. Church, along with northern black organizations, collected food, clothing, and money for the contrabands. One member of the church, excited by the aid program, suggested that teachers, "both colored and white," be sent to the refugees to teach them self-reliance and the value of hard work. These suggestions prefigured the work of the A.M.E. in the South.[6]

2   In April, 1863, the Baltimore Annual Conference of the A.M.E. Church convened with Bishop Payne presiding. Two years earlier, city authorities had refused to allow the conference to meet, because its bishop lived in Ohio and could not legally enter a slave state. To get around this restriction, the church assured city officials that the conference would be held without Bishop Payne, and permission was granted. When the conference opened in 1863, city officials did not attempt to prevent it from meeting. This session of the Baltimore Annual Conference was to be a momentous event in the history of the A.M.E. Church. Doors that had been closed since 1822 were to be opened again by events in South Carolina.[7]

During the course of the conference, the Reverend C. C. Leigh of New York City, a minister of the Methodist Episcopal Church, called upon Bishop Payne. Leigh asked Payne if he had any ministers who were available for missionary work in the coastal areas of South Carolina, which had been taken by the Union army. Payne responded positively to Leigh's re-

5. *Christian Recorder*, October 4, 1862.
6. *Christian Recorder*, March 29, 1862; December 2, 1862; December 27, 1862; March 22, 1862.
7. Smith, *A History of the African Methodist Episcopal Church*, 46.

quest. "The field is yours; go and occupy it," Leigh then told him. Two young A.M.E. ministers, James Lynch and J. D. S. Hall, volunteered to go to South Carolina and work with the freedmen. They were the vanguard of an "army" that would spread across the South gathering black souls for the glory of God and the A.M.E. Church.[8]

James Lynch was born on January 8, 1839, in Baltimore. His father was a member of the free black community of that city and a merchant; his mother was a slave whose freedom had been purchased by her husband. Educated at Kimball University, Hanover, New Hampshire, Lynch joined the Presbyterian Church in New York in 1858 and began to study for the ministry. After a brief association with the Presbyterian Church, Lynch resigned his position and moved to Indiana, where he served as minister of an African Methodist Episcopal Church. Why he made this move remains a mystery. It may be that Lynch, like a number of other black clergymen, felt that his talents would receive greater recognition in an all-black church. Some years later, he would change his mind.[9]

In 1860 Lynch was transferred to the Baltimore Annual Conference of the A.M.E. Church. Three years later, he went to South Carolina as a missionary and organized churches in several parts of the state and in Georgia. In 1865 he was appointed editor of the *Christian Recorder*. After holding this position for two years, he resigned from the A.M.E. Church altogether and went to Mississippi as a missionary for the Methodist Episcopal Church, North. Lynch's reasons for leaving the church are unknown, but he was highly regarded in A.M.E. circles. Bishop Payne paid him the ultimate compliment when he said that Lynch could do more good among the freedmen "than a regiment of white preachers." With such commendations and his education and drive, Lynch probably would have become a bishop in the A.M.E. Church had he remained.[10]

James Lynch was not a typical A.M.E. missionary and cannot be considered representative of the men the church sent South. He belonged to a select, college-educated group of ministers who possessed great organizational talents and whose triumph in the field inspired other ministers in

8. *Ibid.*, 51, 52.
9. Shaw, *The Negro in the History of Methodism*, 145–46; Alexander W. Wayman, *Cyclopedia of African Methodism* (Baltimore: Methodist Episcopal Book Depository, 1882), 101–102.
10. Smith, *A History of the African Methodist Episcopal Church*, 46; quoted in Payne's *History of the African Methodist Episcopal Church*, 467.

the church. J. D. S. Hall, Lynch's colleague in South Carolina, seems more characteristic of the A.M.E. missionaries in the post-emancipation South, though little can be said about him other than that he was literate and apparently served competently in South Carolina. For the majority of A.M.E. missionaries, evidence of their work consists largely of lists of names and of the conferences in which they served.[11]

Altogether the church sent a total of seventy-seven missionaries to the South between 1863 and 1870. Because most did not leave records, it is impossible to make statements about the group as a whole, but some personal information does exist for seventeen, or nearly one-quarter, which permits some generalization concerning their backgrounds, education, and abilities. Fourteen came from the Deep South and border states; the other three were northerners. Twelve had been born free men, two had served as indentured servants, and the remaining three were ex-slaves. They were all educated: Those who had not attended college were either self-taught or the recipients of some form of schooling.[12]

The errand which this black phalanx embarked upon would bring thousands of new souls into the A.M.E. Church. In 1861 the Methodist Episcopal Church, South had more than 200,000 black members. Six years later, this number had declined to about 70,000. The A.M.E. Church's membership in 1866 was about 50,000. Ten years later, the church would have over 300,000 members. This phenomenal growth was due to the efforts of the church's missionaries and the desire of the freedmen to change their religious affiliation.[13]

11. This group included R. H. Cain, Henry M. Turner, and T. G. Stewart. Impressions of Hall may be gained from letters which he wrote to the *Christian Recorder* while stationed in the Palmetto State. See for example the issues for June 27, 1863 and March 12, 26, 1864; Smith, *A History of the African Methodist Episcopal Church*, 52.
12. Smith, *A History of the African Methodist Episcopal Church*, 67, 71, 72. Information concerning the education and family background of these seventeen men may be found in several works: Wayman, *Cyclopedia of African Methodism*, contains biographical sketches of the following missionaries: George Washington Broadie, p. 26; Richard H. Cain, p. 11; Augustus T. Carr, p. 32; Jordan W. Early, p. 55; William H. Hunter, p. 85; James Lynch, pp. 101–102; Charles H. Pearce, p. 125; Hiram Revels, pp. 133–34; Anthony L. Stanford, p. 153; Theophilus Gould Steward, p. 155; Henry M. Turner, p. 10. Wright, *Bishops of the A.M.E. Church*, contains sketches of these missionaries: John M. Brown, p. 11; Jabez Pitt Campbell, p. 123; James C. Embry, p. 162; John Wesley Gaines, p. 173; James Alexander Shorter, p. 307; Alexander W. Wayman, p. 357.
13. William W. Sweet, "Methodist Church Influence in Southern Politics, *Mississippi Valley Historical Review*, I (1915), 547–60.

In entering the South, the A.M.E. missionaries conceived of themselves as "obeying the Providence of God rushing foremost into the field of missionary effort, and gathering in the Methodists who were as sheep without shepherds, in consequence of the rage of Civil War." This great responsibility was theirs because the A.M.E. Church was the first organization in the United States to address itself to the needs of the "enslaved, and the self-emancipated freedmen." According to Bishop Payne, the A.M.E. Church had been organized to save the "advanced thought of the colored people from the worst form of infidelity—that which denies the existence of God." Because they were disgusted by the treatment they had received from white Christians, black people might have become atheistic, Payne believed. This possibility was to be averted by the organization of the A.M.E. Church. The church viewed itself as an asylum protecting blacks from the "blasphemous and degrading spirit of caste" which had surrounded them when they worshiped with whites. Within the A.M.E. Church, Negroes could develop and utilize their moral and mental faculties in positions closed to them in the larger society. The A.M.E. Church, therefore, was an instrument of God's providence dedicated to uplifting the black man in America and ultimately throughout the world.[14]

Having been banned from the South for over thirty years, the ministry of the A.M.E. Church looked upon the South as an area ripe for evangelization. "Heaven has graciously opened the way for the spreading of our beloved Zion in that land," wrote the Reverend R. H. Cain. The time had come, asserted Cain, "for the church to spread her curtains, and lengthen her cords, and gather in her long neglected children." No other religious organization in America was "so eminently qualified for [this] work." The black ministers, Cain argued, could "feel and enter into all the sympathies of [their] poor down-trodden brethren. Other teachers and preachers have feelings but not as we feel for our kindred."[15]

14. *Christian Recorder*, August 11, 1866; Daniel Alexander Payne, *The African Methodist Episcopal Church in Its Relations to the Freedmen* (Xenia: Torchlight Co., 1868), 14. See also Bishop Payne's letter "To the National Convention of Colored Citizens of the United States," printed in *Proceedings of the National Convention of Colored Men of America Held in Washington, D.C. on January 13, 14, 15, and 16, 1869*. Payne was a man obsessed with the idea of respectability. In this letter he stressed the importance of northern blacks teaching the freedmen middle-class values. Payne's obsession was also shared by the members of his church; see *The Minutes of the Pittsburgh Annual Conference of the A.M.E. Church, Held in Brownsville, Pennsylvania, April 15 to 20th 1870* (Pittsburgh: W. S. Haven & Co., 1871).

15. *Christian Recorder*, May 30, 1863.

Although the A.M.E. Church was willing to accept financial aid from white charities, it did not want these organizations to work with ex-slaves. Both racial and psychological circumstances demanded that blacks minister to the needs of the ex-slaves. The teachers of the freedmen should be black, the church argued, especially in segregated schools, because in the past Negroes had been educated to look upon their oppressors as a superior race of people whose position in society was inviolate. Current events, the church averred, were proving this idea false; consequently the education of the Negroes "must" reflect this fact and seek to alter "sentiments and feelings" regarding their race. A sound education, moreover, would encourage the freedmen to confide in and respect each other. These lessons could not be learned from white instructors.[16]

In claiming the paramount right to teach the freedmen, the A.M.E. Church did not wish to disparage or impugn the efforts of white ministers. Many of these people, the church believed, were sincere and honest in their efforts to elevate the freedmen—"That is, to bring them out of the house of bondage and bid them God's speed." But black teachers could accomplish this great work faster. In all the requirements of life the white race was far in advance of the black. Awareness of this fact would generate in the black teacher a "spirit of emulation" and he would aim to quicken the sentiments of his pupils and thus narrow the distance between the two races. This sort of dedication could not be expected from the average white teacher because most white Americans were infected with the poison of slavery. White people "in all their intercourse with us, seek to impress on us that we are their inferiors." Writing from Wilmington, North Carolina, one A.M.E. minister reported that the white teachers working with the freedmen there were unfit for their jobs and should be sent home. "They have not the spirit of true missionaries," he noted, "but are full of their pro-slavery notions, and have taken these positions as stepping stones to other objects." The education of black children, he concluded, could not be left in the hands of racists and opportunists. Southern blacks had to be educated to overcome their fear of their servile condition, or they would never be free.[17]

Believing that these problems could be solved, Henry M. Turner proposed that government agencies and charitable organizations working

16. See Chapter IV herein for a discussion of A.M.E. paternalism.
17. *Christian Recorder*, November 28, 1863; April 23, 1864; May 6, 1865.

with the freedmen employ "colored preachers and lecturers, to travel through the South." They would instruct the freedmen on moral, economic, and political issues and those dealing with industrial pursuits. Turner contended that colored men were particularly suited for this work because even the most incredulous southern blacks would not doubt the force of example. Moreover, these black teachers would not be deceived by slavocrats who often confused whites working with the freedmen. In terms of cost, Turner argued, his proposal would be an inexpensive operation. "No sumptuous tables, fine chambers, attractive misses, springy buggies, or swinging carriages" would distract the black teacher, because he would live with his pupils and attend their social events. White men could simply not get this close to their charges. Turner believed that with twenty-five colored men of good common sense and education working to instruct the freedmen more would be accomplished in one year than in five with white teachers.[18]

If this program of Negro education was to succeed, it was important that the whites of the South also be educated. This was particularly true of the poor whites who were described by one A.M.E. minister as "the most miserable specimens of humanity he had ever seen." Physically they were grotesque, he wrote, with "long legs, short bodies, long necks, bullet heads, sway backs, flat breasts, and big bellies, long swinging arms, pendulous jaws, and a countenance in which ignorance and low cunning [seemed] to struggle by turns for mastery." These people in many respects were as much the victims of slavery as black people. In their ignorance they had carried out the wishes of the slaveholders, being no more conscious of their degradation than black field hands. Moreover, their language, manners, and general deportment left a great deal to be desired.[19]

The educational needs of poor white southerners were obvious. To survive in a free South, they would require some form of instruction. But would these people receive a sound education from their former leaders? Bishop Payne thought they would not. If the South was to be changed, he believed, the education of southern youth could not be left in the hands of the old elite. To do so would be to repeat "one of the most mischievous ideas of the South—the clannish or sectional idea." The South had always been too clannish, and the result was a society closed to outside

18. *Christian Recorder*, August 5, 1865.
19. *Christian Recorder*, May 6, 1865.

ideas. Sectionalism had ruined the South and if allowed to happen again, it would "prove hurtful to the future unity and peace of the Republic." To avoid this error, Bishop Payne suggested that the majority of southerners, black and white, be educated in the South, but at the same time "the master minds" of both races ought to be sent to northern schools. There they would be trained in northern sentiments, principles, and habits, after which they would return to the South as "propagandists" of northern values. "It will be necessary," Bishop Payne said, "to train those who are to shape and color the South, on northern soil and under northern influence, in order that all the roots of bitterness which have been growing there, may be eradicated and the whole southern region converted into communities as pure, as powerful, and as noble as Massachusetts."[20]

3   Reports written to the *Christian Recorder* by A.M.E. missionaries working with the ex-slaves reveal that the freedmen had the same aspirations as men born free. That is, they wanted to work and acquire homesteads for themselves and their families. Writing from Norfolk, Virginia, one missionary described the efforts of some of the local people to attain these goals. The ex-slaves lived in "slab-towns," settlements or villages where all of the houses were built of logs and slabs. A large number of men living in these towns worked for the government during the war, and although they often failed to receive the full wages owed them, they continued to labor for the government and were not discouraged by the poor working conditions. Many could not afford to quit because they had "wives and large families of children" to support. When not working, the men used their spare time to improve their homes.[21]

Descriptions of freedmen working and taking care of their families sustained the missionaries' belief that their charges would do right if given the chance. But accompanying this belief was an awareness of the damage slavery had done to the slaves' moral and intellectual development. The Reverend R. H. Cain, one of the A.M.E. superintendents in South Carolina, made the following statment about the freedmen around Charles-

20. Payne, *The African Methodist Episcopal Church in Its Relations to the Freedmen*, 7–8.
21. *Christian Recorder*, October 1, 1864. See also Herbert G. Gutman, *The Black Family in Slavery and Freedom, 1750–1925* (New York: Pantheon Books, 1976), for a superb discussion of the freedmen's attempts to support their families.

ton. "The condition of the freedmen is bad enough, and the destruction among them is very great. That many are lazy, I admit, because they are just like their masters and mistresses; they never worked for their own living, and hence their slaves imitate their former owners. Who is to blame? Many of them are idlers, so are white people. Many of them think that to be free means to be supported by some person else. . . . These same are improvident and spendthrifts." Cain was not totally pessimistic about the freedmen's future. He thought that if they were given the same opportunities as white men, their condition would improve. "Viewing them generally," he wrote, "I find that there is a disposition to work, and get land, possess property, educate their children, and thus elevate themselves and the race to which they belong." As a missionary in South Carolina, Cain would work to make this statement a reality.[22]

When Cain arrived in South Carolina, he was ambivalent about the ability of the freedmen to survive. After working with them for a while, he changed his attitude and wrote to the *Christian Recorder* that "the progress of the freedmen [was] beyond the most sanguine expectations of their friends." The freedmen's "industry, perseverance, and earnestness in working their crops and securing means of comfort are unprecedented." All of their crops were excellent and "everyone is anxious to become independent of the charities of the government as well as the benevolent societies of the North." This spirit of industry, he noted, also prevailed in the Sea Islands, which were "teeming with the rejuvenating influence of free labor, and industrious people." Crops of cotton, rice, sugar, and garden produce were doing well and would have been better had there been more rain. Black people could be seen working "everywhere and at everything" and would have been engaged in more enterprises if they had had the means.[23]

Cain thought that if the government encouraged the freedmen to become small farmers and producers of staples which could be transported to northern cities and abroad, the ex-slaves would be "the most loyal and peaceful citizens in this country." All the freedmen required was encouragement and opportunity. In another example, when a group of ex-slaves

22. *Christian Recorder*, June 17, 1865. For another assessment of the freedmen in South Carolina, see the letter by T. G. Steward to Stribey and Whipple, June 28, undated, in American Missionary Association Papers, Amistad Research Center, Dillard University.
23. *Christian Recorder*, August 19, 1865; September 30, 1865.

in Georgia learned that the government was not going to give land to the
freedmen, they sought and found gainful employment. Henry M. Turner,
a missionary in Georgia, reported that the blacks in Liberty County had
acquired a great deal of property through hard work. Some were so successful that they even employed whites on their farms.[24]

The ease with which the ex-slaves acquired property and got established depended to a great degree on what their former masters thought
of blacks' asserting themselves. Some planters would not make arrange-
ments with their ex-slaves to plant and share crops. Instead they waited
until crops had been planted and were about to be harvested, and then
resorted to fraud and force to deprive the freedmen of the fruits of their
labor. Failing deception, they turned to violence. An A.M.E. missionary
working in Wilmington, North Carolina, described the treatment of freedmen living in and around the city. "Some are driven from their cabin and
cultivated field, occupied during the absence of its owner. The contracts of
others, for its brief possession are continually broken, and they are de-
prived of the promised reward of their labor . . . some are violently beaten
or rudely scourged: (many cases have just occurred). Some are deliber-
ately shot down in open day on the public streets, (among them a girl,
because she was unwilling to return to the wretched home of her former
master, who is now in jail awaiting trial)."[25]

Not all planters were so cruel and some did sign contracts with their
ex-slaves. In Georgia many of the former slaveholders had contracts
drawn up which paid male workers ten to fifteen dollars a month. Women
were paid five dollars a month plus rations. Writing from Charleston,
R. H. Cain reported that the conditions of black people there were improving. "The planters are contracting with the freedmen," he said, "for
the coming year, and the latter hope to realize something handsome for
the agreement." Cain's report was not completely sanguine, however. Although some of the planters tried to work out agreements with their former slaves, others continued to treat the freedmen callously. Hundreds of
ex-slaves were driven from their homes when they refused to accept the
contracts offered by their former masters. Compelled to seek homes elsewhere, they were exposed to want and often arrested as vagrants.[26]

Their difficulties did not quench the freedmen's thirst for education,

24. *Christian Recorder*, August 19, 1865; November 4, 1864; June 18, 1874.
25. *Christian Recorder*, September 2, 1865.
26. *Christian Recorder*, February 24, 1866.

however. The desire among the freedmen to be educated was very strong. A female member of the A.M.E. Church teaching in Norfolk wrote to the *Christian Recorder* that the schools there had been closed since July "but the interest hitherto manifested by the pupils, has not diminished. . . . So earnestly have they entreated me that I could not refuse to grant their request, to keep my school open during the summer." George W. Broadie, a missionary in Raleigh, North Carolina, on entering a church in that city, found it filled with adults and children. "From four hundred to five hundred were present; both white and colored. Some acting in the capacity of teachers."[27]

Henry Turner, the missionary who was to play a prominent role later in Georgia politics, wrote the following about the black residents of Smithville, North Carolina: "The colored people are anxious to have schools established here. They seem to have a high appreciation of the beneficial advantages of education." The people, Turner said, "recognized the power of education, despite the limited capacity hitherto allowed to their intellectual development." Several people had asked if his wife would come and teach in Smithville. He told them it would be impossible because he had not heard from her in three months; moreover, if she were detained as long as some of his papers and letters had been on the way, it would take six months for her to reach Smithville. In Georgetown, South Carolina, three men, formerly slaves but now landowners, did not wait for outsiders to come and establish schools. They employed a local white man—a "southerner of culture and refinement"—to teach their children and paid him a hundreds dollars a quarter.[28]

In general, the white southerners encountered by A.M.E. missionaries seemed to have mixed feelings about blacks' being educated. One missionary in South Carolina found a planter teaching a "colored school." The planter had built the school on his own property, the missionary said, and seemed to enjoy his work. He told the black minister that he "was not obliged to do it, but felt it would be better for all if the people were educated." This act of philanthropy was not an isolated incident. Writing some years after Reconstruction, Theophilus G. Steward recalled the generosity of some planters in the town of Marion, South Carolina. Steward described the planters as being wealthy and kind. One of them, a Major Gibson, donated land for Steward's church. Another, Colonel Du-

27. *Christian Recorder*, February 6, 1864; September 17, 1864; August 19, 1865.
28. *Christian Recorder*, February 25, 1865; January 9, 1873.

rant, provided timber for the church's construction, and other whites in the community contributed money for the building. Some white people in the town, however, were not pleased with the new conditions and tried to impede his work, to the point of setting fire to a temporary building. While their church was being constructed, the congregation worshiped in an old building given to them by one of the planters, and during the week this structure served as a school. The burning occurred soon after the blacks occupied the site. Steward's opponents seem to have been against both the idea of a Negro church and the idea of a Negro school. Any institution which attempted to uplift blacks was an anathema as far as they were concerned. In Hopkinsville, Kentucky, the white residents opposed schools for blacks, even Sunday schools. A missionary visiting the town wrote to the *Christian Recorder* that "colored children [were] not allowed the privilege of day or Sunday schools." Hundreds of black children were to be seen running in the streets, because they were not allowed to take books into their hands. Prior to his visit, the minister said, a local "colored lady" had tried to open a day school, but the whites "broke it up" and forbade the blacks to have any school. Incidents such as this did not deter either the freedmen or the ministers of the A.M.E. Church.[29]

Working with the freedmen required a great deal of patience and tolerance. Most A.M.E. missionaries seem to have possessed these qualities. They did not consider the freedmen their racial and cultural inferiors, as did some of the white missionaries. A.M.E. missionaries explained the freedmen's shortcomings in environmental terms rather than racial ones. Slavery, they thought, was the cause of their people's lack of refinement, subservient behavior, and distrust of each other. Time and education, the black missionaries believed, would resolve these problems and change the freedmen's religious attitudes.[30]

4 Before the Civil War, the religious life of slaves depended to a great degree on the piety of their masters. If the masters were not religious or believed that religion spoiled slaves, they tried to prevent their bondsmen

29. *Christian Recorder*, January 9, 1873. Theophilus G. Steward, *Fifty Years in the Gospel Ministry* (Philadelphia: A.M.E. Book Concern, 1921), 67–68; *Christian Recorder*, October 14, 1865.
30. Elizabeth Ware Pearson (ed.), *Letters from Port Royal, 1862–1868* (1906; reprinted New York: Arno Press and New York *Times*, 1969), 75, 82, 180, 241; *Christian Recorder*, February 21, 1863; March 10, 1865.

from attending services. These planters feared that their servants would imbibe dangerous ideas at religious meetings, especially if these gatherings were not supervised by whites. The Nat Turner Rebellion of 1831 confirmed an idea latent in the mind of many planters, that religious instruction made slaves restive and dissatisfied.

Slaves with pious masters were encouraged to lead Christian lives. Some planters took their servants with them to church, where the slaves sat in a special part of the church called the "nigger pew" or "heaven." Lorenzo Ezell, a slave in Texas, described the seating arrangement in his master's church: "De Baptist church have a shed built behind de pulpit for cullud folks, with de dirt floor and split log seat for de women folks, but most de men folks stands or kneels on de floor." This arrangement had but one aim, to impress upon the slaves their inferiority to whites—even in the house of God. White ministers with black parishioners preached the text "servants be obedient to your master." Slaves who were recalcitrant were told that "he that knoweth his master's will and doeth it not, shall be beaten with many stripes." Some slaves were spared the humiliation of having to sit in segregated sections of white churches, though the black congregations were supervised by whites who made certain that nothing was said to undermine the institution of slavery. Commenting on the planters' idea of religious instruction for slaves, Henry Bibb observed that it had "driven thousands into infidelity. They view themselves as suffering unjustly under the lash, without friends, without protection of law or gospels, and the green-eyed monster tyranny staring them in the face. They know that they are destined to die in that wretched condition, unless they are delivered by the arm of omnipotence. And they cannot believe or trust in such religion as above named."[31]

Not all of the slaves were driven to this position. Although the planters tried to control the religious life of their slaves, they were not totally successful. Some slaves, for example, questioned their master's intepretation of the scriptures and countered it with one of their own. Believing that God was both compassionate and just and that he had not abandoned them, slaves conducted religious services in secret. In the slave quarters,

---

31. Quoted in Norman R. Yetman (ed.), *Life Under the Peculiar Institution* (New York: Holt, Rinehart and Winston, 1970), 112; Gilbert Osofsky (ed.), *Puttin On Ole Massa* (1847; reprinted New York: Harper and Row, 1969), 69. John A. Scott (ed.), *Journal of a Residence on a Georgia Plantation in 1838–39 by Francis Anne Kemble* (1863; reprinted New York: Alfred A. Knopf, 1961), 92, 106, 107; Yetman, *Life Under the Peculiar Institution*, 13.

late at night, or in "brush arbors" located in the fields and woods, a number of bondsmen worshiped God without white supervision. One slave recalled that his master "didn't like for us niggers to pray." To get around these obstacles, they held prayer meetings in the cabins. "We'd set on the floor and pray with our heads down low and sing low." The slaves met once or twice a week in different locations when they wanted to hold a "real meetin' with some real preachin'." This distinction between "real" meetings and preaching and that prescribed suggests that not all were passive in the face of religious indoctrination. A number of bondsmen transcended the instructions implicit in the injunction "servants obey your masters" and were able to see the tenuousness of their owners' position. They were aided in this process by the insights which they derived from the moralistic message of evangelical pietism. Slaves who did this were exercising an inner freedom which allowed them to see the paradoxical position which they occupied in southern society.[32]

Most planters who catechized their slaves were either Baptists or Methodists, and these sects required their members to lead unblemished lives. Adherents were urged not to lie, steal, cheat, or fornicate. Moreover some masters who were both harsh and Christian told their slaves that a failure to adhere to these proscriptions might mean death. But certain conditions of plantation life worked against the normalization of the preached morality. The greatest threat to this system of social control came from the planters themselves who violated its precepts by heavy drinking and sexually exploiting female servants. The examples set by these masters undermined their bondsmen's faith in what they were taught. Perceptive slaves could see the difference between practice and theory. In short, the moral transgressions of the masters turned their plantations into spiritual wastelands, which encouraged religiously emancipated slaves to interpret Christianity for themselves and reinforced other forms of resistance born of desperation. Slaves on some plantations lied to their masters simply in order to survive. On other plantations, when rations were low, a slave mights have to steal food so that his family could live.[33]

Before the A.M.E. missionaries arrived in the South, the slaves had de-

32. Quoted in *Slave Narratives: A Folk History of Slavery in the United States from Interviews with Former Slaves* (Washington: The Library of Congress Project Works Projects Administration for the District of Columbia, sponsored by the Library of Congress, 1941), 16, 240; also quoted in Yetman, *Life Under the Peculiar Institution*, 13.
33. Osofsky, *Puttin On Ole Massa*, 77; Charles Stearns, *The Black Man of the South and the Rebels; The Characteristics of the Former, and the Recent Outrages of the Latter*

veloped their own conceptions of God and Christianity. Although the services of the bondsmen were often conducted in secret, an outsider might on occasion be privileged to hear or witness one of these meetings. From their descriptions and the testimony of ex-slaves, a picture of these gatherings may be constructed. Slave religious meetings were characterized by a great deal of emotional fervor. Singing, shouting, and dancing were common. Sermons, when preached, often explored the theme of "chosenness." Slaves who could read drew parallels between their condition in the South and that of the Israelites in Egypt. This was not escapism but a form of typology: that is, they used the scriptures to understand their position in history. Having freed the Hebrew children and delivered Daniel from the lion's den, God would save them too. God, the slaves believed, was accessible to all and in heaven there would be no class or racial distinctions. Indeed, God had sent his son into the world to save those who would recognize him as their savior. And in a world torn by strife and misery, Christ had taken a particular interest in the plight of the downtrodden. In a sermon preached to a congregation of Georgia slaves in 1851, a slave preacher named Bentley emphasized Christ's concern for the poor:

> I remember on one occasion, when the President of the United States came to Georgia and to our town of Savannah. I remember what an ado the people made, and how they went out in big carriages to meet him. The clouds of dust were terrible, and the great cannon pealed forth one salute after another. Then the president came in a grand, beautiful carriage and drove to the best house in the whole town, and that was Mrs. Scarborough's! And when he came there he seated himself in the window. But a cord was drawn around the house to keep us negroes and other poor folks from coming too near. We had to stand outside and only get a sight of the president as he sat at the window. But the great gentlemen and the rich folks went freely up the steps and through the door and shook hands with him. Now, did Christ come in this way? Did He come only to the rich? Did He shake hands only with them? No! Blessed be the Lord! He came to the poor! He came to us, and for our sakes, my brothers and sisters![34]

(1872; reprinted New York: Negro Universities Press, 1969). See Chapter 33 for an admirable discussion of slave religion. The slaves did not accept their masters' definition of right and wrong according to this account.

34. Yetman, *Life Under the Peculiar Institution*, 75. For the importance of typology in Amer-

Sermons like this one and slave songs gave the religion of the slaves an
apocalyptic vision. This was particularly true of the spirituals, which were
filled with imagery drawn from the history of the Hebrew children. The
adventures of these Old Testament heroes profoundly affected the slaves'
thought, as Lawrence W. Levine has suggested. All of these biblical char-
acters, Levine observes, "were delivered in this world and delivered in
ways which struck the imagination of the slaves." The impact of these
biblical events can be seen in the lyrics of the spiritual:

> O My Lord delivered Daniel,
> O why not deliver me, too?

> He delivered Daniel from de lion's den
>   Jonah from de belly ob de whale,
> And de Hebrew children from de fiery furnace,
>   And why not every man?

To slaves the occurrences described in these verses were not abstractions.
They were real and suggested that God had not abandoned them. They
would be redeemed and their oppressors punished. This point was made
by a North Carolina slave, who commented that even the most ignorant
bondsmen thought that their enslavement was unjust and would not last
forever. "God," they said, "will bring them to an account." The slaves'
belief that they would be saved was manifested in the fervor of their religious services.[35]

The enthusiasm which the slaves displayed in worship amused and re-
pelled whites who saw their services. But to the slaves, shouting, groan-
ing, and dancing were ways of releasing tension and at the same time a
way of communication with God. "You gotta shout and you gotta moan
if you wants to be saved," one slave declared. Being saved was important
to the slaves because they knew that after all of the toil and trouble they
had endured on earth, a world of peace awaited them in heaven. To the

ican history, see Ursula Brumm, *American Thought and Religious Typology*, trans. John
Hoaglund (New Brunswick: Rutgers University Press, 1970), 23; and Adolph B. Ben-
son (ed.), *America in the Fifties: Letters of Fredrika Bremer* (1853; reprinted New
York: Oxford University Press, 1924), 132–33.
35. Levine, *Black Culture and Black Consciousness*, 49; William Francis Allen, *et al.*, *Slave
Songs of the United States* (1867; reprinted New York: Peter Smith, 1951), 94; Thomas
P. Fenner, *Cabin and Plantation Songs* (New York: G. P. Putnam's Sons, 1874), 193;
John W. Blassingame (ed.), *Slave Testimony* (Baton Rouge: Louisiana State University
Press, 1977), 135.

slave, heaven was the antithesis of what he experienced on earth. It was a beautiful place beyond the sky, with "golden streets, and a sea of glass upon which Angels danced and sang in praise of God, who sat upon a throne of gold." In heaven there would be no sun to burn their backs or slave drivers to lash them. Heaven was a place of never ending peace where families would be reunited.[36]

The initial reason the A.M.E. Church appealed to the freedmen had little to do with either its theology or worship. A.M.E. missionaries attributed their success among the freedmen to consanguinity. "We had the blood," one of them wrote. "The fires of oppression have melted the Anglo-Africans into one, it has burnt up their wrath and jealousies, and whenever they see each other's face, they see the countenance of a brother." R. H. Cain, the A.M.E. superintendent in South Carolina, stated that "the blacks recognize in our organization the idea of nationality of manhood. They feel the time has come for the black man to take his place as a free man." These statements only partially explain why southern blacks joined the A.M.E. Church. They do not provide a complete explanation of the sudden changes of denomination prevalent among southern blacks after the Civil War. The primary reason was the desire on the part of the ex-slaves to test their freedom. Being free meant they could choose their own church. This decision would no longer be made for them by "old Massa." Moreover, in a society in which religion played a prominent role, church membership and attendance were signs of respectability. To be without a church affiliation was to occupy a second-class status in many southern communities. Therefore, when a slave left his master's church, he took an important step in defining himself as a free man and as a responsible member of the community in which he resided.[37]

5 A.M.E. missionaries who went South to work with the freedmen learned that the task would not be easy. Commenting on the problems

36. Quoted in Lawrence W. Levine, "Slave Songs and Slave Consciousness: An Exploration in Neglected Sources," in Hareven (ed.), *Anonymous Americans: Explorations in Nineteenth Century Social History*, 120; Keith Winsell, "Evolution of Religion Among Negroes in Antebellum America" (Unpublished seminar paper, University of California, Los Angeles, 1967), 4.
37. Quoted in Tanner, *An Apology for African Methodism*, 369; *Christian Recorder*, September 29, 1866.

that these men faced, Bishop Wesley Gaines wrote, "There was much to contend against from both white and colored. The former noted a movement the independence of which grated upon them under so recent defeats and losses. . . . Then there was a prejudice born of generations, of the recognized dominance of the whites which we had to meet and overcome in leading bodies of negroes to seek a church where they could be free and untrammeled in their religious worship."[38]

The first two A.M.E. missionaries to encounter these conditions were James Lynch and J. D. S. Hall. Arriving in South Carolina late in May of 1863, they began working with the freedmen living around Port Royal, Edisto, and Beaufort in the Sea Islands. Initially, Lynch worked on St. Helena and Ladies Islands and Hall ministered to the freedmen around Beaufort City, Port Royal, and Hilton Head islands. The difficulties that these two encountered suggest that the success of an A.M.E. missionary depended on more than his ability to preach. To succeed in the South, an A.M.E. minister had to be a politician, organizer, public relations man, fund raiser, and shepherd of his flock. Above all, these ministers could not be dogmatic or inflexible. To gain converts for their church, they had to accommodate themselves to local customs.[39]

Writing from Beaufort late in June, Hall described one of his communion services. When "I was about to consecrate the elements, I saw two white brethren, who I thought were preachers. I gave an invitation to the preachers, if there were any in the house, to come around the table." Three ministers came forward, he said, and one of them helped him serve communion. During the course of the service, over one hundred people communed, "and at every table succeeding the first row there were from three to five or six persons communed." In opening the communion services to whites, Hall was following the A.M.E. tradition. In the South, this policy would be pursued to allay any fear southerners might have about the church's work among the freedmen. Underlying this fear was the fact that ex-slaves were joining the A.M.E. Church "very rapidly." In ten days, Hall wrote from Beaufort, "we number nearly seventy. I have married four couples, buried two, one of whom was Robert Smalls, Jr., baptized twenty-six, of whom five were infants, and nineteen grown persons." Elev-

38. Quoted in Gaines, *African Methodism in the South or Twenty-Five Years of Freedom*, 13.
39. Payne, *History of the African Methodist Episcopal Church*, 469.

en of these adults requested that they be immersed rather than sprinkled and Hall assented to their request, thus showing his tolerance of local custom and previous religious affiliation.[40]

Writing from the Sea Islands at the same time, James Lynch noted that he and his co-worker had organized churches at Beaufort and Hilton Head. "I expect before three months," Lynch wrote, "we will have organized a dozen societies. My own heart has been fired by our brethren here. Ignorant though they be on account of long years of oppression, they exhibit a desire to hear and learn, that I never imagined. Every word you say while preaching they drink down and respond to with an earnestness that sets your heart all on fire, and you feel that it is indeed God's work to minister to them."[41]

Lynch's description of his work in the village of Helenaville provides an interesting picture of how A.M.E. ministers approached the freedmen and became a part of their community. The town contained about eight hundred "colored inhabitants" and was surrounded by plantations. There were two churches in the town and Lynch and his congregation occupied one of them; the other was used for storage. Before the war, Lynch's church had belonged to a congregation of white Episcopalians, but after the commencement of hostilities they fled and the "colored people" inherited the town and churches. The blacks were divided denominationally into Methodist, Presbyterian, Baptist, and Episcopalian, "all having equal rights and worshipping together, or what is nearer the truth, quarreling together." This was the state of things when Lynch arrived in the settlement.[42]

Since the townspeople thought the natural state of a black man was subservience, the appearance among the ex-slaves of an educated and self-confident black preacher must have been traumatic for them. Nevertheless, Lynch was successful in dealing with these people. On "the first sabbath I preached to them," Lynch wrote, "they began to wonder among themselves as to what denomination I belonged." Never having heard of the A.M.E. Church, the freedmen were said to have been in a quandary. Lynch informed them that he was a minister of the A.M.E. Church sent by General Saxton, "and as such I organized the church under our disci-

40. *Christian Recorder*, June 27, 1863.
41. *Ibid.*
42. *Christian Recorder*, July 25, 1863.

pline." The majority of the mixed congregation voted to join the A.M.E.
Church, with only a few Baptists dissenting. The people of Helenaville
responded positively to Lynch's preaching, and on the next Sunday, when
he announced a quarterly meeting for eleven o'clock, "the house was
crowded at nine a.m." Accompanying the birth of the A.M.E. Church,
Lynch wrote, "there was a birth of souls in the kingdom of Christ." On
this occasion, he baptized 25 adults, received into the church 153 new
members, and administered the sacraments to an even larger number.
The next night (Monday), Lynch held a quarterly conference. "Twelve
brethren met," he reported. "Only two of them knew what a Quarterly
conference was, or what it was to make a motion; a little instruction and
patience soon made them understand it." He also licensed two local
preachers and two exhorters who had been previously verbally licensed.
(The licensing of ex-slaves as preachers by A.M.E. ministers in the field
was to create considerable controversy in the church.) Lynch also preached
to the ex-bondsmen living on plantations situated around the village and
ministered as often as he could to the spiritual needs of the "colored"
regiments stationed near Helenaville. There were four black regiments
nearby and only one had a chaplain. On several Sundays, after preaching
two services in his church, Lynch walked to a nearby military camp and
preached to the troops. Along with his ministerial duties during the week,
Lynch ran a day school with 142 scholars. Most of the teaching in the
school was done by two women teachers, one of whom was Lynch's
sister.[43]

While Lynch and Hall were working in the Sea Islands, the Reverend
Alexander Wayman, an A.M.E. minister stationed in Baltimore, moved
southward into Virginia. Born September, 1821, in Carolina County,
Maryland, he worked on his parents' farm as a child and was taught to
read and spell by his father. Utilizing these skills, he taught himself how
to write. Wayman's limited educational background did not hurt his career in the A.M.E. Church. He joined the church in 1840 and held several
offices in the hierarchy before being elected a bishop in 1864. Wayman's
mission to Virginia was prompted by an appeal from the black members
of the Butte Street Methodist Episcopal Church, South, of Norfolk, Virginia, who worshiped in a chapel named St. John's. During the course of

43. *Ibid.*

the Civil War, the blacks became dissatisfied with their relationship to the white Methodists and decided to withdraw from the M.E. Church, South, when Union forces occupied Norfolk. On May 4, 1863, the official board acquired title to the church. Both moves on the part of the blacks in Norfolk seem to have been fairly easy. In several other instances, withdrawal would be both complicated and expensive. The congregation of St. John's were able to make their moves quickly because they were aided by a Union officer, Major General Dix, who was stationed in Norfolk.[44]

Five months after leaving the M.E. Church, South, the trustees of St. John's agreed to unite with the Baltimore Annual Conference of the A.M.E. Church. They were influenced in the decision by a Professor Woodbury, superintendent of the Government School in Norfolk, who promised the trustees that he would obtain an A.M.E. minister to organize the church. In Baltimore, Woodbury secured the services of Wayman, who was at the time an elder in the Baltimore Annual Conference. He came to Norfolk and conferred with the members of St. John's, who then voted to adopt the discipline of the A.M.E. Church. To celebrate the occasion, Wayman preached a sermon which was to become famous among A.M.E. ministers and would be used by many of them later on to bring other churches into the A.M.E. fold. The sermon was titled "I Seek My Brethren." The activities of the A.M.E. missionaries in the Sea Islands and Virginia were preludes to a larger endeavor.[45]

Bringing the word of God to the freedmen was not an easy task. A.M.E. missionaries were not wealthy, and in some states, as in Georgia, the railroads refused to allow black preachers to travel at reduced rates. Poverty and prejudice made missionizing difficult, and the ministers had to travel either by foot or on horse. On one of his tours, Henry M. Turner recalled, he covered five hundred miles, "travelling night and day, stopping here and there trying to preach." Traveling on rural southern roads, the missionaries were sometimes harassed by local whites. Riding to an appointment somewhere in the South, the Reverend Jordan Winston Early was overtaken by a white man who ordered him to surrender as a runaway slave. Early refused the request but agreed to accompany the slave catcher

44. Wright, *Bishops of the A.M.E. Church*, 35.
45. Israel La Fayette Butt, *History of African Methodism in Virginia* (Norfolk: Hampton Institute Press, 1908), 32–3.

to a nearby magistrate's office. Upon arriving at their destination, they were met by a mob of armed men who insisted that Early be detained and held until he could prove his identity. He told them he could not be detained without a warrant from an officer of the government. The magistrate agreed with him. Early says he knew that the men were well armed and would give him trouble if he acquiesced to their demands. While the mob retired to a tavern for a drink, Early was left alone with the magistrate. "I gave the squire a sign of the Masonic fraternity," Early stated, "which he acknowledged, and I showed him my papers from the government and my native state." The magistrate then allowed Early to proceed on his way. After a delay of several hours he was able to reach his destination on time and preach to a large assembly that night. When Early's experience is compared with that of other A.M.E. ministers, he appears to have been fortunate. Upon arriving at his mission he found his congregation assembled and waiting, which suggests that they either possessed a church or were wealthy enough to rent a hall. In either case Early was more than fortunate—he was blessed. He did not have to worry about building a church or wresting it from vindictive whites, enraged at the thought of blacks' having their own church.[46]

In some towns, A.M.E. ministers working in the South had to build their churches. For example, James Lynch reported that in the village of Mitchelville, South Carolina, he had a congregation of three hundred members without a church building. After working with the congregation for a while, he left to attend the annual conference of the A.M.E. Church. When he left "they were getting out the frame of the church. On my return I found that they had raised this frame and were waiting for lumber to finish it." Lumber was both scarce and expensive on the Sea Islands, and Lynch's parishoners could not raise enough money to complete their church. It was important that the church be finished, Lynch said, because his work was threatened by a "certain source"—the M.E. Church, North. Accordingly, Lynch purchased the necessary lumber at a cost of $266.40. In his absence the trustees of the church had raised a hundred dollars enabling Lynch to make a down payment and sign a note for the remainder which was to be paid in sixty days. The note was accepted on his endorse-

46. Tanner, *An Apology for African Methodism*, 35; Sarah J. Early, *Life and Labors of Rev. Jordan W. Early*, ed. George A. Singleton (Nashville: A.M.E. Sunday School Union, 1894), 51–52.

ment, and the ex-slaves completed the exterior construction. The church was not yet finished: "We have to get boards for flooring, window sashes, doors, seats and lamps. We have got to do some painting and would like a melodeon," Lynch wrote. To complete his church Lynch appealed to some of his colleagues with wealthy congregations. But his appeal fell on deaf ears, and he had to complete his church with local resources. The problems Lynch faced were typical of those of other A.M.E. ministers.[47]

A missionary working in Jollife, a village located fifteen miles outside of Portsmouth, Virginia, wrote to the *Christian Recorder* and requested help because the windows, doors, and seats had been removed from a church which he wanted to use. Before the Civil War, the minister reported, the church had been used jointly by "colored people, Indians, and white people." When the war broke out the "white minister left, and the whites would not allow the colored people and Indians to worship in the house, nor would they worship there themselves, particularly after the Yankees came here." Before the A.M.E. minister's arrival, the blacks had tried to reopen the church but they were unsuccessful. The white stewards who controlled the building in the minister's absence refused to accede to their request and kept it closed. This was the state of affairs when the minister arrived. "On the sixteenth of this month (August) I sent forward a notice, that I should preach in the Jollife meeting house on the next day, at one o'clock P.M. On the morning of the 17th, I called on the steward, J. R., a white man and told him of the appointment, and asked if he intended to eject us. He said, certainly not. When asked how about the other stewards? He said surely no one will disturb you." When the blacks arrived at the church, they found it stripped of doors, windows, and furnishings. Winter was coming, and if they wanted to use the building it would have to be closed. The minister estimated that it would cost one hundred dollars. It was a small amount, but his congregation of ex-slaves was poor, many members were unemployed, and they could not raise the funds. When the government refused to help his congregation "fix a denominational house," he could only appeal to the ministers of well-to-do congregations in the A.M.E. Church to help him and his flock.[48]

Although most congregations experienced financial difficulties building their churches, not all of the congregations organized by A.M.E. min-

47. *Christian Recorder*, August 13, 1864.
48. *Christian Recorder*, September 3, 1864.

isters were poor or destitute. The Reverend R. H. Cain, for example, built a church in Charleston which cost $10,000 and seated 2,500 people. The church was built by black laborers and designed by Robert Vesey, the son of Denmark Vesey. Most construction projects, however, went less smoothly than the one in Charleston. Writing about his experience in Lumpkin, Georgia, Theophilus G. Steward described a situation which required a minister with organizational talent. Prior to Steward's arrival, the congregation had made arrangements to purchase a lot, but nothing had been paid on it. They also had tried to purchase an old church which their white coreligionists had abandoned. "The building was sold to the colored people," Steward wrote, "for one-hundred and fifty dollars, providing they move it off the ground within a definite time." When he arrived in Lumpkin the time had nearly expired. The people had made no preparations to move the building "but on the contrary were sitting down apparently helpless and hopeless."[49]

Shortly after he arrived on July 7, 1867, Steward opened a school. He also informed his congregation that the church building would be moved on August 1, 1867. With the date of removal announced, Steward proceeded to prepare his congregation for the transition. He called together a number of young men and they agreed to furnish shingles for the roof. The nails for the roof were to be provided by a society of children especially organized for that purpose. He also organized a women's society to furnish the house with "new windows." When the day arrived, the building was "cut into sections and carried by men from its old site to the new one, and there re-erected." Two ex-slave carpenters directed this operation. By September 12, the church was moved, re-erected, a new roof put on it, new windows installed, and the lot was paid for. Steward proudly boasted that all of this had been accomplished in two months and five days after his arrival. His success in Lumpkin was repeated by A.M.E. ministers in other parts of the South.[50]

6   Competition from ministers of other denominations blunted the A.M.E. Church's success. Writing from Augusta, Georgia, James Lynch reported that he had received into the A.M.E. connection a large black

49. *Christian Recorder*, October 14, 1865.
50. Steward, *Fifty Years in the Gospel Ministry*, 94.

congregation formerly associated with the M.E. Church, South. This accession was exceptional, however, for the church's minister, the Reverend Samuel Drayton, also joined the A.M.E. Church. Most black ministers of the M.E. Church, South remained opposed to the work of the A.M.E. Church. Lynch praised both the pastor and his church. The church property, he said, was worth eight thousand dollars. Moreover, the church was out of debt, and the deed to the property was drawn up so that there was "no likelihood of any question being raised as to the rights of property." Associated with the church were several small branches located in the surrounding countryside which also followed the parent church into the A.M.E. organization. Lynch also announced that in Atlanta the Trinity Methodist Episcopal Church had joined the A.M.E. Church "by an overwhelming majority." Both churches had withdrawn from the M.E. Church, South because they were persuaded by Lynch. They may also have been motivated by a sense of patriotism. In Nashville, for example, two black congregations associated with the M.E. Church, South decided to leave that organization and gave the following reasons for withdrawing: "A vast majority of the ministers and members of the Methodist Church, South have proven themselves disloyal to the constitution and Government of the United States by identifying themselves with those who are now in open rebellion against it." It was their duty as "Christians and citizens to bear testimony against such unjustifiable conduct."[51]

Whether their reasons were racial or patriotic, or a combination of both, the freedmen seem to have been attracted to the A.M.E. Church. Henry M. Turner, a presiding elder in Georgia, said that he had received five hundred persons into the A.M.E. Church in less than a month. This number did not include the work of his subordinates. When the two figures were combined, Turner said, the membership in his department came to "five thousand and three hundred immortal souls." The following month he reported that he and his ministers had taken in eleven thousand new members. Five thousand of these Turner claimed to have brought in himself. In a letter written to the church's paper several months later, he called 1866 a year of revivals in Georgia. Some A.M.E. Churches in the state had as many as 450 probationers on their rolls, he claimed. People who were formerly thought immovable had been brought into the church

51. *Christian Recorder*, July 8, 1865. Quoted in Payne, *History of the African Methodist Episcoal Church*, 471.

and "powerfully converted." The growth of the church in Georgia was so phenomenal that Turner had to redistrict his field of labor. Serving under him were ten elders; to each of these he gave a subordinate district or precinct, over which they were to have full control, subject only to his correction. Ministers working with the freedmen in other states reported similar successes.[52]

In expanding in the South the A.M.E. Church did, however, encounter obstacles. The opposition of some southern whites to A.M.E. missionaries has already been mentioned, but the church also had to contend with the obstructionist tactics of the M.E. Church, North. On May 9, 1865, Bishop Payne, accompanied by Elder James Handy and licentiates James H. A. Johnson and Theophilus G. Steward, sailed from New York to Charleston, South Carolina. Handy was to return north and Johnson and Steward were to remain in the South to work with the freedmen. For Bishop Payne, his entry into the city of his birth was a triumph. Thirty years earlier, he had been forced to flee Charleston for teaching free black children how to read and write. On May 16, Bishop Payne, assisted by his traveling companions James Lynch and William Bentley, a local preacher, organized the South Carolina Conference of the A.M.E. Church. The meeting was held in the "colored Presbyterian Church" because the A.M.E. Church did not own a building in the city. These six men were the only persons present at the opening session of the conference. They were soon joined by elders R. H. Cain and Anthony S. Stanford, from New York and Philadelphia; George S. Rue, from the New England Conference; and four local brethren. The establishment of schools, the conference's committee on education reported, "had demonstrated the natural capacity of the colored race and done much to make the white people of the North believe in the equality of the natural capacity of colored persons with white." In the South, the report disclosed, education was "the great safeguard of the people. Without, ingenious and designing men would make them tie themselves; and cry amen to measures detrimental to their vital interest."[53]

The black Methodists of Charleston opened their hearts to the A.M.E.

52. *Christian Recorder*, July 7, 1866; August 11, 1866; November 24, 1866; August 10, 1867; see the *Christian Recorder* for these dates for other missionary successes: September 17, 1864, June 3, 1865, April 6, 1867, and October 12, 1867.
53. Payne, *History of the African Methodist Episcopal Church*, 469; *Christian Recorder*, June 3, 1865.

Church. "Many old mothers, bending towards the ground, came to the conference every morning, and listened with rapturous delight to their deliberations," Cain wrote to the *Recorder*. "When the conference was over, they would come forward and embrace us, and pour blessings upon us, and even kiss our hands."[54]

The entry of the A.M.E. Church into Charleston was opposed by Theodore W. Lewis, a minister of the Methodist Episcopal Church, North, who was in Charleston as its representative. In late November of 1863 the War Department had delegated to Edward R. Ames, senior bishop of the M.E. Church, North, "an authority deemed to be of great importance to the nation in its efforts to restore tranquility . . . and peace." Applicable to the military districts of Missouri, Tennessee, and the Gulf, the War Department directive placed at the disposal of Bishop Ames those churches of the M.E. Church, South which were pastored by rebels. Acting under these instructions, Lewis had expropriated the property of the M.E. Church, South in the Sea Islands and Charleston. Lewis' first encounter with A.M.E. ministers in the Sea Islands had resulted in a stand-off, with James Lynch and J. D. S. Hall not at all deterred by Lewis' claims of authority. He therefore decided to make his stand in Charleston, where the stakes were much higher. When the South Carolina Annual Conference of the A.M.E. Church convened, Lewis sent Bishop Payne and his cohorts a letter welcoming them to the city. They reciprocated the honor, and Lewis then invited Bishop Payne to hold his ordination service in Trinity Church, one of the black churches under his jurisdiction. During the course of the service, however, Lewis became apprehensive upon "seeing the impression it made on the minds of the members." When the service was over, Cain recalled, Lewis "called them all down into the basement and harangued them with a tirade of abuse against the A.M.E. Church." In addressing his own congregation, Lewis told them to ignore the A.M.E. Church and "wait until things became more settled," and reminded them "that the A.M.E. Church was based on the distinction of color." Given the history of these two churches, this was an ironic statement for a white M.E. Church minister to make. Continuing, Lewis told his flock that the A.M.E. Church was another denomination and "that in the North there was no distinction in the M.E. churches; that colored people have the

54. *Christian Recorder*, June 3, 1865.

same rights and privileges as the whites, and that if they left him they would lose their church property, that the property belonged to the M.E. Church, and that he would hold it for that body."[55]

Although the M.E. Church may have been color-blind in the North, Lewis made certain that in Charleston it adhered to local customs. "He has given the colored people the old churches," R. H. Cain wrote, "and reserved New Bethel for the whites, yet tells them they are equal to the whites in all things. But, if the colored people go to New Bethel Church, they must go up into the gallery as they formerly did."[56]

Despite its difficulties with Lewis, the A.M.E. Church was able to organize the black Methodists of Charleston and the state at large. One year after its founding, the South Carolina Annual Conference reported a membership of 22,338 members.[57] Bishop Payne presided at the conference and ordained forty itinerant ministers, fourteen of whom were elders. He also appointed seven superintendents "to plant and train mission churches"; Anthony S. Stanford and Henry M. Turner, for Georgia; George W. Broadie and Samuel B. Williams, for North Carolina; Augustus T. Carr and R. H. Cain, for South Carolina; and Charles H. Pearce for Florida and Alabama.[58] These men and their subordinates covered a great deal of territory. Three years after the church entered the South, the *Recorder* reported that A.M.E. churches had been established in Norfolk, Portsmouth, and Richmond, Virginia; Wilmington, Raleigh, and Newbern, North Carolina; Charleston, Hilton Head, and Beaufort City, South Carolina; Savannah, Augusta, Macon, and Atlanta, Georgia; Mobile, Alabama; Vicksburg and Natchez, Mississippi; and in Nashville and Memphis, Tennessee. In addition to these urban centers, circuits were established along the James, Cohambie, Ashley, and Cooper Rivers; on the Sea Island of South Carolina; in Georgia from the Chattahoochee to the sea; along the Cumberland to the Mississippi; and from the Mississippi to the Rio Grande.[59] In 1867 three conferences were formed out of the original mission territory of the South Carolina conference, in North

55. Quoted in Ralph E. Morrow, *Northern Methodism and Reconstruction* (East Lansing: Michigan State University Press, 1956), 33. Smith, *A History of the African Methodist Episcopal Church*, appendix, 505; *Christian Recorder*, June 3, 1865.
56. *Christian Recorder*, June 3, 1865.
57. Smith, *A History of The African Methodist Church*, 508.
58. Payne, *History of the African Methodist Church*, 470.
59. *Christian Recorder*, June 9, 1866.

Carolina, Georgia, and Florida. A year later this process was repeated in Alabama, Mississippi, and Texas. Three other conferences organized in 1868, Kentucky, Tennessee, and Arkansas, completed the organization of the South. In a short period of five years, the A.M.E. Church had been able to expand throughout the South.[60]

7 The difficulties which the A.M.E. Church experienced with the M.E. Church, North were predictable because before the two churches entered the South they had been rivals. What A.M.E. missionaries did not anticipate was black resistance to their work. From the reports to the *Christian Recorder* it is apparent that A.M.E. missionaries were startled by the reception they received from southern black preachers. A number of these clergymen perceived A.M.E. ministers as their enemies and refused to have anything to do with them and their church. Professions of brotherhood by A.M.E. ministers were rebuffed. Henry Turner told the Georgia Annual Conference of the A.M.E. Church that he had found "a few colored preachers who were sternly opposed" to the A.M.E. Church. These ministers told Turner that they wanted to organize a "conference under the auspices of the M.E. Church, South, but we [the A.M.E. Church] were gobbling them up." Moreover, they said that if they joined the A.M.E. Church, "they would not be able to catch up in fifty years, and consequently they would have to be lackey boys for us." Turner denied these charges and told the ministers that the A.M.E. Church would not oppress them. This incident is revealing because it shows how these men perceived the A.M.E. Church. Their reference to being "gobbled up" suggests that they saw the A.M.E. Church as an all-consuming Leviathan—a monster which would devour them and their congregations. Such fears did have some basis in fact; that is, the ministers were correct in thinking that if they joined the A.M.E. Church their positions might be lost. Many were uneducated and had never been ordained. They held their positions at the sufferance of the M.E. Church, South, which was not known for its advocacy of an educated black clergy. To cover up their deficiencies, some of the ministers took preposterous titles, calling themselves "elder deacon" and "elder bishop." They attempted to impress their followers and to

60. Bucke (ed.), *The History of American Methodism*, II, 536–37. For the growth of the church in Virginia, see the *Christian Recorder* for January 14, 1865.

offset what they thought were the impeccable credentials of their A.M.E. rivals. The strategy had a limited utility, and when it failed they adopted other tactics.[61]

Southern black preachers used a variety of strategems to keep A.M.E. ministers out of their churches. An A.M.E. minister serving in Baton Rouge, Louisiana, reported that the local preacher told him if he did not leave his church, "he would take a stick and beat [him] out." Another minister stated that he was verbally assaulted in the pulpit of a New Orleans church by twenty irate women who were led by a character nicknamed "Emperor Williams." Williams demanded that the minister surrender the pulpit but the minister refused. Although comic, this incident does illuminate an important fact—opposition to the A.M.E. Church came from both the local preachers and some of their followers.[62]

In a number of churches the congregations divided, with some members favoring the A.M.E. Church and others championing the M.E. Church, South. In Nashville, an A.M.E. minister conceded considerable trouble in holding on to his church, with a number of leading members returning to the M.E. Church, South. "There are about twenty of these backslides [sic], and they are trying to get the property, because it was deeded to white trustees belonging to that body," he said. Another minister working in Nashville told a similar tale of betrayal. He identified his church as Andrew's Chapel and stated that the congregation tried to purchase the building from the M.E. Church, South. While these negotiations were in progress, some of the colored people told the ministers of the M.E. Church, North that if they would buy the property the congregation would join the M.E. Church, North. The purchase was made, and the minister and his followers found themselves without a church. In another church located in Little Rock, Arkansas, some of the congregation refused to part with their old preacher. They told the A.M.E. minister sent to serve them that they were "opposed to an educated ministry" and to "northerners coming among [them], seeking offices, and assuming the most prominent positions."[63]

All of this suggests that a number of the freedmen were opposed to the A.M.E. Church and that they saw the church as their enemy and in some

61. *Christian Recorder*, December 15, 1866; September 10, 1864.
62. *Christian Recorder*, December 17, 1864; September 10, 1864.
63. *Christian Recorder*, May 19, 1866; February 4, 1871.

cases decided to associate themselves with white Methodist churches—
thinking probably that in these churches they could keep their old ministers and style of worship. They knew that in the A.M.E. Church some of
their traditional religious practices (corn songs or ring shouts, for example) would have to go. This was the only conclusion they could draw
from the emphasis which the A.M.E. Church placed on education. On
one occasion when some southern black preachers were presented to an
A.M.E. bishop for ordination, he refused to perform the rite. He told
their sponsors that he could not ordain a man unable to read or write.
After some discussion, the bishop changed his mind, when it was explained to him how much the church needed these men and their help. In
1866 the Georgia Annual Conference of the A.M.E. Church refused to
"pass a man for orders who could not read." This was a curious decision
because they were "not particular as to his writing," an observer remarked. The desire of the A.M.E. Church to have an educated clergy is
understandable, but the church seems to have gone out of its way to insult or alienate potential southern members. For example, at the 1868
meeting of the General Conference, there was opposition to the seating
of delegates from the South. If the conference had followed "the constitution then in force for fifty years," these delegates would not have been
seated. The conference, Bishop Gaines said, "wisely and justly saw the
work they represented must be recognized" and decided to alter its rule.[64]

Despite the opposition of some southern blacks, the A.M.E. Church
did not relax the literacy requirement it had established for ministers. If
they were to be successful in the South, their ministers had to be able to
read and write. Henry M. Turner told some of the ministers in his district:
"We cannot expect the people to feed, clothe, and reverence us unless we
are able to repay them with that instruction and knowledge which our
exalted position demands, and they naturally expect. The simple titles of
preacher, deacon, and elder are not enough to satisfy those who are thirst-
ing for moral and religious knowledge. We must be able to impart the
same, otherwise . . . our preaching will be little more than the low of an

64. "Corn songs" was the name given to "ring shouts" by the hierarchy of the A.M.E.
Church. Ring shouts were the counterclockwise, shuffling dance which slaves danced
during and after their religious services. See *Nation*, May 30, 1867, pp. 432–33, for a
description of a ring shout; Early, *Life and Labors of Rev. Jordan Early*, 64; *Christian
Recorder*, December 15, 1866; Gaines, *African Methodism in the South or Twenty-Five
Years of Freedom*, 16–17.

ox or the bray of an ass." This attitude was shared by James Lynch, who stated that he had met some freedmen who told him that "if the northern preachers do not know any more than we do, we can do without them." To make sure that this did not happen, ministers serving in the South were urged to engage in private study. In some conferences they were required to bring a "written article on some specified topic" to the meeting. These papers were read and criticized by the bishop and other members of the conference on a day set aside for this purpose.[65]

Obviously, then, image was an important factor in the church's missionary work. To win new converts, it was essential that A.M.E. missionaries be exemplars of the ideas which they preached. As Christ's representatives on earth they had to be "able, learned, and chaste." Their daily lives were to manifest that discipline which Richard Allen believed was requisite for Negro uplift. Emulation of this behavior would bring the freedmen out of darkness.[66]

Financing this program of brotherhood and uplift was not easy. The A.M.E. Church was not wealthy and on several occasions Bishop Payne appealed to northern philanthropists for aid to support the church's missionary work. These requests for help were not always successful, and the church had to rely on its own slim resources. Ministers serving in the field complained that they could not do their jobs properly because the church was not managing its resources properly. This was James Lynch's complaint in a letter to the *Christian Recorder*. "It is a lamentable fact," wrote Lynch, "that the African Methodist Episcopal Church is not more active in pushing into the southern fields." Lynch noted that there were black people in Virginia, Tennessee, and northern Alabama who would gladly welcome A.M.E. ministers but that none had been sent. He attributed this failure to a poor use of manpower. The church's preachers were poorly distributed in the conference districts. In some places three men were doing the work of one, which made it difficult to find enough men to work in the South. Lynch blamed these failures on the church's hierarchy.[67]

65. Gaines, *African Methodism*, 61–62; *Christian Recorder*, September 9, 1865; Early, *The Life and Labors of Rev. Jordan Early*, 54.
66. Gaines, *African Methodism in the South or Twenty-Five Years of Freedom*, 16–62; see, for example, the advice given to some Georgia ministers by Bishop Brown, 34–35.
67. Daniel A. Payne, *Recollections of Seventy Years*, 150. In some instances A.M.E. missionaries' salaries were paid by the American Missionary Association; see the letters

Many of the church's elders were unwilling to leave their comfortable charges and go to neighboring towns to organize new churches. Elders stationed in border states, Lynch thought, should leave their churches in the hands of local preachers "and go a hundred miles, if need be, to plant a church." The behavior of the church's bishops also exasperated Lynch. Not one of the bishops of the A.M.E. Church, he claimed, had visited a seceded state since the war began, except at three points: Norfolk and Portsmouth, Virginia, and Nashville, Tennessee. This lack of initiative on the part of the bishops could also be seen in other areas. The bishops, he declared, "have never . . . sought from competent military authority, that protection of our interest and recognition of our influence as gives prestige and power." In this charge, he may have been referring to the harassment of A.M.E. congregations in Louisville, where the Union army closed black churches and flogged black people found on the streets after dark. Lynch may also have been criticizing the bishops for failing to protect the rights of black ministers traveling in the South. While traveling on a boat in South Carolina, for example, Lynch was forced off the upper deck by a white man who told him he did not belong there (though Lynch protested and was allowed to ride where he pleased). Problems like these only made the southern work more difficult. The bishops seemed to be more interested in traveling to California, where the church was well established, than in helping the freedmen along the Mississippi and the Gulf. Other ministers working in the South complained that they worked hard to establish churches and schools only to find that their appeals for books and disciplines were unanswered. Letters send to the secretary of the missionary society and to the editor of the *Christian Recorder* were ignored.[68]

Indifference and mismanagement caused some of the brighter ministers to leave the A.M.E. Church. The withdrawal of James Lynch has already been noted. Several years later another prominent missionary, Anthony L. Stanford, general book steward of the A.M.E. Church, deserted to the M.E. Church, North. Born and educated in Springtown, New Jersey, Stan-

---

from T. G. Steward to George Whipple, July, undated, 1865; T. G. Steward to George Whipple, November 10, 1865, in American Missionary Association Papers, Amistad Research Center, Dillard University.
68. *Christian Recorder*, February 11, 1865; April 5, 1862; September 24, 1864; February 11, 1865; October 14, 1865; June 17, 1865.

ford taught school briefly and joined the A.M.E. Church in 1858. He served in several conferences of the church and for a short time edited the *Christian Recorder*. In 1869 he was elected general book steward. Two years later he left the A.M.E. Church and went to Mississippi, where he joined the M.E. Church, North. Stanford's defection to the enemy camp probably created a stir in the A.M.E. Church. Alexander Wayman in his *Recollections* notes that Stanford's "admission into the M.E. Church, North was hailed with delight: But when they found him out his dismissal was hailed with more delight." Just what Stanford did to warrant expulsion is not known. After his expulsion he went to Africa and practiced medicine. The examples of Lynch and Stanford did not create a stampede, but other ministers did leave the A.M.E. Church, and the primary reason they gave for leaving was lack of support.[69]

Defections by some of their colleagues did not deter the majority of A.M.E. ministers. They had come south, Turner said, seeking their brethren for the purpose of elevating them, and this task could not be abandoned because of a paucity of funds. In many of the towns and villages where A.M.E. ministers established churches, the inhabitants could barely take care of themselves. To support a missionary would have been an added burden. In these locales A.M.E. missionaries became laborers and worked beside the people they came to help. A bond was created with the local people, and the missionaries experienced some of the trials and tribulations of their parishioners. Not all freedmen were mired in poverty; some possessed property but were short on cash. In these situations ministers were paid in chickens, eggs, etc. In the Alabama Conference, for example, these items could be accepted as salary. A minister who could not adjust his style to these conditions did not succeed.[70]

Despite its difficulties, the A.M.E. Church did reach large numbers of freedmen who responded to its program of uplift and discipline, but the rapid expansion of the church into the South was fraught with problems. The incorporation of new members into the A.M.E. Church created difficulties for the church's hierarchy. Many of the new members were accustomed to worshiping in an exuberant style which A.M.E. clergymen

69. Wayman, *Cyclopedia of African Methodism*, 153; Payne, *Recollection of Seventy Years*, 183; *Christian Recorder*, January 9, 1873.
70. *Christian Recorder*, September 21, 1867; February 3, 1866; April 18, 1868; Edward W. Lampton, *Digest of Rulings and Decisions of the Bishops of the A.M.E. Church from 1847 to 1907* (Washington: Record Publishing Co., 1907), 151.

found distasteful. This attitude on the part of the ministry suggests that by the 1870s the aggressive spirit which characterized the church's creation had become attenuated. This may partly explain the church's failure to support its missionaries. Further, although the church was poor, poverty alone cannot explain this failure. Forces beyond the church's control undermined its mission to the freedmen. In short, the great quest was only a qualified success.[71]

71. See, for example, *Minutes of the Eighth Annual Session of the Virginia Conference of The A.M.E. Church, April 15, 1874* (Richmond: Ferguson & Rady Printers, 1874), 7; *Christian Recorder*, February 20, 1873; Early, *The Life and Labors of the Rev. Jordan Early*, 124.

IV "We Would Like to Have All the Ground"

The A.M.E. ministers who went south to work with the freedmen were dedicated to the principle of Negro uplift. Two closely related ideas motivated them: first, they believed their church had "been and [was] an instrument in the hands of God to lift [their] race up from degradation." Second, they thought this work should be done by blacks and only by those who were members of the A.M.E. Church. Such beliefs predisposed the hierarchy and ministers of the church to look with displeasure on the efforts of other religious organizations working with the freedmen. Jabez P. Campbell, an A.M.E. bishop, made the position quite clear when he remarked, "We would like to have all the ground." His desire was not to be fully realized. Emancipation made the South a missionary field, and representatives of other northern churches and philanthropic organizations flocked south to reap the harvest of emancipated souls.[1]

In the war-torn South competition for the freedmen's religious preference was to be stiff. Competing with the A.M.E. Church were the Methodist Episcopal Church, North; the Methodist Episcopal Church, South; the African Methodist Episcopal Zion Church; the Colored Methodist Episcopal Church; the Roman Catholic Church; and the American Missionary Association, which was financed by Northern Congregationalists. Although all of these organizations were interested in elevating the southern black man, this mutual concern led to some rather unchristian behavior on the part of their southern emissaries. Antagonisms between men of God took a variety of forms: racial, intraracial, interdenomina-

---

1. Smith, *A History of the A.M.E. Church*, 520. Quoted in Morrow, *Northern Methodism and Reconstruction*, 135.

tional, denominational, sectional, and political. These squabbles suggest that the rhetoric of uplift disguised a power struggle.

The major antagonists in the contest for black souls were the A.M.E. Church and the M.E. Church, North. The rivalry dated back to the end of the eighteenth century, when northern white Methodists had raised the barrier of "caste" in the house of God. Members of the church learned an important lesson from their difficulties with M.E. Church, North: Black men could not expect to assume roles of leadership in a church controlled by white men. All power, glory, and achievement in such an organization would be the white man's. But with the organization of the A.M.E. Church in 1816 black people had a church which would utilize their talents. Its existence was proof, members of the church believed, that black men did not have to depend on their white brothers for moral instruction or tutelage in any facet of life. As a symbol of black independence, cooperation, and elevation, the church had played a prominent role in developing a positive sense of self among northern blacks. Once the slave power was destroyed, the church's program could be carried to the freedmen.[2]

The desire to aid the freedmen was also present in several other northern churches, and when the first A.M.E. missionaries arrived in the South they found the field already occupied by ministers of the M.E. Church, North. The white church was rich and well organized, and it possessed powerful friends in the federal government. Impelled by a sense of mission similar to that which propelled its black rival, the M.E. Church, North wanted to transform the South. A cultural and political transformation would be possible once the Confederacy was defeated and the section purged of its sins. In the carnage of the Civil War the hierarchy of the M.E. Church, North saw a divine purpose. God was wreaking upon the South his "inevitable vengeance against sinners." He had chosen the North to be the instrument of his justice against a people who condoned "man buying, woman whipping, maiden debauching [and] children selling." Cleansed, pacified, and chastened, the South would reenter the Union as a productive partner. On the debris of the old South a new Beulah land would be erected and the M.E. Church, North intended to

2. See Chapter I herein for a discussion of the difficulties. Quoted in Jenifer, "What Has African Methodism to Say as to Its Past? What Has It to Offer the Present? What Does It Promise the Future?", 253.

play a central role in its creation. The hierarchy of the church realized that the process of southern regeneration was not to be accomplished solely by force of arms. Once the fighting ceased, a new psychological struggle would replace it. Once heresies of secession, states' rights, and slavery were extirpated, a new moral and religious social system would follow. Ministers of the M.E. Church, North believed that they were the agents of southern reeducation and redemption and that other religious organizations were incapable of doing the job.

Not altogether altruistic in its desire to redeem the South, the M.E. Church, North hoped to recover ground lost during the era of sectional conflict when it had been torn apart by the slavery question. The northern Methodists wanted to reincorporate into their fold all of those southerners who had joined the M.E. Church, South in 1845. Now that the original divisive issue was dead, the northern churchmen thought their errant brothers should reunite with them. This goal received a great boost in November of 1863, when the War Department gave the church a warrant allowing it to occupy all of the "houses of worship" belonging to the M.E. Church, South which were pastored by disloyalists. Initially the order was applicable only to the military department of Missouri, Tennessee, and the Gulf. Union soldiers serving in these districts were instructed to aid the church in its program of property acquisition. Later on, when those areas of the Confederacy which were exempted by the original order came under Union control the church was empowered to act there. Although the authorizations were never fully enforced, they did contain immense potential for aggrandizement. A number of the ministers of the M.E. Church, South were Confederate sympathizers, and the possibility that they would use their pulpits to disseminate treasonous ideas was the government's rationale for turning the property of southern Methodists over to the M.E. Church, North. But in giving this authority to the northern church, the government unwittingly placed it on a collision course with the African Methodists.

1   In 1860 the M.E. Church, South had over 200,000 black members. Most of the church's black parishioners were organized into segregated congregations that were pastored either by white or by slave preachers who were supervised by elders of the parent church. Although nominally under black Methodist control, the buildings of worship were in fact reg-

istered as property of the M.E. Church, South. The edifices had been paid for by the blacks but the deeds to the properties were held by the southern white Methodists. The government decision to allow the M.E. Church, North to occupy the property of the southern church also gave it control of the black congregations of the M.E. Church, South.

Disturbed by this decision, James Lynch, serving in South Carolina, wrote to Secretary of War Edwin M. Stanton and asked him if the government intended to enforce the order allowing the M.E. Church, North to occupy the property of disloyal southern Methodists. The Secretary of War informed Lynch that President Lincoln had "revoked all orders issued from the War Department to religious denominations, not conceiving it to be the duty of the government to run churches. The people in any part of the states in rebellion were therefore to determine their own church relations." The first preacher or congregation to acquire an abandoned church was to have title to it until the war was over and civil law became operative again. This decision heartened A.M.E. missionaries because they wanted to elevate their southern brothers and acquire the property which the black Methodists had paid for. The M.E. Church, North identified itself with the party of antislavery to such an extent that southerners saw the northern church as a political organization and discounted its religious mission. Rebuffed by their white brothers, the northern churchmen turned to the blacks.

An initial ambivalence toward southern blacks reflected a division within the M.E. Church, North over missionary policy. Some northern Methodists thought that their church should be color blind in its missionary endeavors. Their opponents thought that a program which did not make allowances for southern racial attitudes would not succeed. Traditionally, they argued, southern whites and blacks had worshiped separately and to mix the races indiscriminately in the same church would be "hazardous and dangerous." They suggested instead that the freedmen be allowed to join the African Methodist. The resistance of white southerners undermined this position and the church turned to the freedmen. The church's efforts to win black converts was not to be half-hearted: four-fifths of the money it expended in the South during Reconstruction would go for this purpose.[3]

3. This discussion of northern Methodism is taken from Morrow, *Northern Methodism and Reconstruction*. See also William W. Sweet, *The Methodist Episcopal Church and the Civil War* (Cincinnati: Methodist Book Concern, 1912), and "The Methodist Epis-

The decision to work with the freedmen signaled the outbreak of hostilities between the M.E. Church, North and the A.M.E. Church. The first encounter in this struggle for souls took place in the Sea Islands of South Carolina. James Hall, stationed at Hilton Head, reported to the *Christian Recorder* that in his absence a minister of the M.E. Church, North had tried to steal his congregation. Hall told the paper that he had left his station for several weeks in order to procure books and supplies for the school he was establishing and during his absence a minister of the white church tried to establish a congregation among the people of the village. Upon his return, Hall said, he met with his people and "made all the necessary inquiries." One member of his flock told him that the "white brother had been doing all that he could to get them." The villagers, however, had not been swayed by the white minister's blandishments but informed him that they would do nothing until Hall returned. Undaunted by this response, the white missionary went to the military officer in command of the district, informed him of conditions in the village, and claimed that the villagers wanted him rather than a colored minister to preach for them.[4]

Hall's next confrontation with a minister of the M.E. Church, North occurred at Beaufort, South Carolina. One morning while he was in his room, two ministers of the white church called on him. T. W. Lewis of Worcester, Massachusetts, told the black minister that he had been sent to Beaufort by Bishop James of New York and that he was empowered by the War Department to take charge of the Methodist churches in that district whose pulpits were not "filled by loyal white ministers." He was also instructed by his bishop to make Beaufort his headquarters. When Lewis demanded to know by what authority Hall was there, the black minister replied that he was in Beaufort under the auspices of the Baltimore Annual Conferernce and the National Freedmen's Relief Association. Lewis told his opponent that he did not want to interfere with his work, but that he would, nevertheless, push forward the interest of the M.E. Church, North. After a heated exchange on the merits of their respective organizations, the two ministers agreed that Hall would preach

---

copal Church and Reconstruction," *Journal of the Illinois State Historical Society*, VII (1914), 147–65. For a discussion of the pre–Civil War split between the northern and southern branches of Methodism, see Mathews, *Slavery and Methodism*; *Christian Recorder*, June 25, 1864.

4. *Christian Recorder*, November 14, 1863.

in the local church on Sunday mornings and Lewis in the afternoons. This agreement did not settle their differences. Several days later Lewis returned to talk with Hall, but nothing was resolved.[5]

In their final encounter Lewis proposed a plan that he thought would harmoniously conclude their difficulties: He was to occupy the church for part of the time and Hall the other. On Sundays, when he was preaching, Lewis wanted to officiate at both the morning and evening services. This rule was also to apply to meetings held during the week. Hall found the proposal unacceptable and told Lewis that he would "not [be] unequally yoked together with a white man." The proposition, he asserted, was good for his rival but not for him because all of the "war power" was on his adversary's side. In arguing this position, Hall recognized that the authority given the M.E. Church, North by the government was superior to that which he enjoyed. If their dispute over control of the church culminated in a showdown, he would be the loser. Rather than continue the argument, Hall decided to withdraw from the field. His withdrawal signaled an escalation in the war for southern church property and souls.[6]

Within the A.M.E. Church, Hall's departure from Beaufort was viewed with anything but equanimity. On April 2, 1864, the church's official paper published an article whose title asked the question: "Is There to Be Any Unpleasant Conflict Between the Methodist Episcopal Church and the African Methodist Episcopal Church?" The piece criticized the way Lewis had treated Hall. Especially vehement about the questions the white missionary had asked his black counterpart, the article described his queries as "too strong for a minister of Christ." The column went on to say that Hall's treatment suggested that the loyalty of black men was questionable or "that [whatever they did] must be done in a subordinate position." Nor could Lewis' behavior be rationalized by saying that he was only carrying out a government order. The government, after all, was asking black men to defend the Union. Did it propose to reward them by dispossessing "their preachers of pulpits thrown open to them by their own race and to which they were invited as teachers?" Recent events, the paper concluded, suggested that the misunderstanding between the two churches could be satisfactorily resolved. Taking note of the fact that the general conferences of both churches were scheduled to meet at the same

5. *Christian Recorder*, March 12, 1864.
6. *Christian Recorder*, March 26, 1864.

time in Philadelphia, the *Christian Recorder* urged them to take advantage of the occasion to sign a "treaty of reciprocity."[7]

Thirteen months after the conferences adjourned, the paper claimed that an agreement had been signed. The two churches, it announced, had decided in the future to maintain "amicable relations." To insure this amity, the M.E. Church, North had offered to give the A.M.E. Church twenty thousand dollars to finance its southern work. In addition, the white church was giving up its plans to minister to the freedmen, thereby leaving the rich crop of black souls to be harvested by the A.M.E. Church. Later events were to show that the A.M.E. Church was naive to expect either aid or "amicable relations" with its rival. The M.E. Church, North was not interested in helping the black Methodist, and this agreement appears to have been a tactical move designed to put the Negroes off guard.[8]

When missionaries of the white church encountered their black counterparts in the field they often taunted the blacks with the wealth at their disposal. This led the black clerics to conclude that if the white church had so much money it should be willing to share it with a poor relative. Was not charity one of the hallmarks of a good Christian? In supporting the A.M.E. Church, the blacks reasoned, their coreligionists would be furthering God's work. The A.M.E. Church, they pointed out, was the first Methodist organization to commence operations in the South. Moreover, it had a history of operating missions in those parts of the United States where free blacks were allowed to worship without restrictions. Now that providence had opened up a new field for its missionaries, who would hinder them? The officers of the church, therefore, asked the M.E. Church, North to finance their missionary campaign. J. P. Campbell, the A.M.E. bishop in charge of missionary work in the Mississippi Valley, stated the proposition eloquently when he remarked: "We . . . did hope that as the mother . . . of Methodism had means without men, and the African M.E. Church . . . had men without means . . . our mother would furnish the means, and let us furnish the men." In requesting aid from

7. *Christian Recorder*, April 2, 1864.
8. The general conferences were scheduled to meet on the first Monday of May, 1864. This explanation of what transpired while the conferences were in session is questionable and subsequent events cast doubt on the veracity of the stories. See the *Christian Recorder* for July 22, 1865.

their competitor and the sole right to minister to the freedmen, the black hierarchs did not think that they were doing anything untoward.[9]

Although a few ministers in the M.E. Church, North may have been willing to aid the black church, the majority were not. Lewis, for example, continued to harass A.M.E. missionaries. In Savannah he told a congregation of black Methodists whom James Lynch was endeavoring to bring into the A.M.E. Church that "it was dangerous for them to come out of the Methodist family." Lynch's retort was so persuasive however, that the members of the church voted overwhelmingly to join his organization. The important thing about this conflict, though, is not that the black minister won. The central issue was Lewis' implication that the A.M.E. Church was not part of the Methodist family. His comment reflected an attitude which a number of ministers in the M.E. Church, North would come to adopt. Their antipathy was fueled by a sense of superiority.[10]

To offset the monetary advantages enjoyed by their white Methodist brothers, A.M.E. missionaries appealed to the freedmen's sense of consanguinity. Blood, they claimed, was stronger than money. Given this fact, they argued, the M.E. Church, North should restrict its activities to southern white Methodists and leave the ex-slaves alone. Bishop Campbell of the A.M.E. church, when asked why he had come South, replied: "I own I went South to gather up all the colored Methodists I could find. I thought this right belonged to us, and I went after them. I thought the ministers of the M.E. Church would gather up all the white Methodists in the South as theirs. Nor could I object to their taking all the colored Methodists, who of their own free choice wished to unite with them."[11]

As far as the hierarchy of the black church was concerned, the task of working with the freedmen clearly belonged to them because the M.E. Church, North would not treat the freedmen equitably. To make this point clear, the A.M.E. Church tried to show the white Methodists how prejudiced they were. Spokesmen for the A.M.E. Church did not condemn the efforts of the M.E. Church, North in the South. Hoping to dissuade their white brothers, they commended them for making a "magnificent Chris-

9. *Christian Recorder*, March 12, 1864; April 2, 1864; quoted in Morrow, *Northern Methodism and Reconstruction*, 135.
10. *Christian Recorder*, January 21, 1864; Morrow, *Northern Methodism and Reconstruction*, 135.
11. *Christian Recorder*, September 21, 1867.

tian" effort. "We watch with gladden hearts" one black churchman exclaimed, "the progress of the M.E. Church towards an enlightened policy in dealing with our people." These sweet words, however, prefaced a scathing analysis of the white church's racial policies. "The M.E. Church still proscribes its colored ministers, and members by legislation, administration, and custom, throughout its bonds, to a greater or lesser extent. We regret to say not withstanding its wonderful energy in behalf of the freedmen, in dealing with black men ecclesiastically, it is behind the Episcopal and Presbyterian Churches, that make no boast of the radical element. Colored ministers cannot sit as actual or honorary members of all the Annual Conferences of the M.E. Church." The charge of racial discrimination, always a strong weapon in the A.M.E. arsenal, won for them a number of new converts.[12]

Noting this success, white missionaries decided to use the same tactic against the A.M.E. Church. In Charleston, for example, they told the Methodist community that the A.M.E. Church was an organization based on distinctions of color. The accusation that the black church excluded whites and mulattos from its ranks was widely disseminated in the city. R. H. Cain, the A.M.E. elder stationed there, believed that the tactic was discouraging prospective members and doing the church great harm. He urged the South Carolina Annual Conference of the A.M.E. Church to deny the canard. The conference issued a denial which declared: "That we hail all men as our brothers, whatever be their complexions, and we have ever maintained, that ours is a church without distinctions of color, accepting gladly all men who believe in Christ, and work for the elevation of our race." Concurring in these sentiments, Bishop Payne told the people of Charleston that the A.M.E. Church did not exist for the purpose of separating colored men from white men. His church, he said, was for all men. When prejudice passed away, the Bishop observed, "and white men and colored could worship at a common altar, the A.M.E. Church and the M.E. Church would be one." His statements may have allayed the fears of the Methodists in Charleston, but their effect on the M.E. Church, North seems to have been negligible.[13]

An A.M.E. missionary stationed in Vicksburg, Mississippi, told his superiors that the bishops and ministers of the M.E. Church, North were doing all they could to distract the minds of the colored Methodists, to

12. *Christian Recorder*, April 21, 1866; August 22, 1868.
13. *Christian Recorder*, June 3, 1865.

prevent them from joining the A.M.E. Church—"telling them that they [had] plenty of money, and [would] build churches for them and preach to them for nothing." These offers were hard to pass up and some freedmen looking for a new church accepted them. In the struggle for members nothing could be left to chance. Where money failed, complexion might succeed, and when combined the two could, it was thought, work miracles.[14]

To disprove the charge that it was a racist institution, the M.E. Church, North began ordaining blacks and sending them South. Initially the church licensed thirty men to preach to the freedmen. When compared with A.M.E. ministers, they were not well educated: only four could read and none could write. Possessing only the rudest elements of an education, they made up for this difficulty by being spirited evangelists. The message they brought to the ex-slaves was hot and unadorned. In sending out such emissaries, the M.E. Church, North may have been trying to capitalize on the southern black's taste for "spirit" and not "larnin" in religious matters. The church may also have been trying to outflank its black competitors by allowing its new communicants to give full vent to their emotions.[15]

The A.M.E. Church did not approve of emotional outbursts at its services. Ministers and members were instructed to approach the altar of God decorously. Loud singing, shouting, and gesticulations, the A.M.E. clergy thought, were atavistic practices which did nothing to advance the race. This sort of behavior, they believed, only contributed to the public's negative perception of blacks. Civilized people did not behave this way in church, the racists would say. The black missionaries also opposed such conduct because it kept alive superstitions which, they claimed, were detrimental to the freedmen's uplift. If the ex-slaves were to become model citizens, they would have to be educated to the ways of freedom. But having come South to perform this task, A.M.E. missionaries found their path blocked by the M.E. Church, North. A.M.E. efforts to dissuade the white church from its course did not succeed. The M.E. Church, North continued to evangelize the freedmen and disregard the A.M.E. Church's appeals for help.[16]

Upset by the discord, one of the M.E. Church, North's missionaries

14. *Christian Recorder*, March 24, 1866.
15. *Ibid.*; Morrow, *Northern Methodism and Reconstruction*, 145–47.
16. *Christian Recorder*, May 19, 1866.

suggested in October of 1866 that the two churches unite. "Prejudice should be dismissed," he said, "and a true christian spirit cultivated." Within the A.M.E. Church the suggestion evoked a mixed response. An editorial in the church's paper hailed the idea and observed that the two churches were moving closer each day. The initial enthusiasm was not shared in any great degree by the church's missionaries, only two of whom seem to have favored the project. The white church, these two pro-unity spokesmen argued, was wealthy, and if their colleagues had access to its resources they "could gather up and save thousands of black people who otherwise might be lost." Moreover, the Catholic Church was attempting to win black converts in the West and Southwest and their efforts must be stopped. Finally, a union with the M.E. Church, North would strengthen the Methodist movement among blacks. The present state of affairs tended only to "weaken Methodism among the colored Methodist of [the] country." The example set by the A.M.E. Church, they hoped, might persuade the A.M.E. Zion Church to join the union with the result that all the black Methodists in the country would be united.[17]

The two missionaries who endorsed union were roundly criticized by their colleagues. Union with the M.E. Church, North, one critic said, would destroy something God had created in "his wise providence." The A.M.E. Church provided the black man in America with an arena in which he could exercise his "talent, education, and grace." How was he to do this in a church dominated by white people? The black man's position in the new church would be secondary because the two churches did not have equal resources. To push for union, given these conditions, was naive and it would create more problems than it would solve. Instead of uniting with the M.E. Church, North, they should try to combine with the A.M.E. Zion Church. United, these two black churches could work miracles among the freedmen. Nothing came of this suggestion because it was as far-fetched as the proposal to unite the A.M.E. Church and the M.E. Church, North.[18]

The escalating hostility between the A.M.E. Church and its white rival baffled R. H. Cain, the A.M.E. elder stationed in South Carolina. Cain wrote to the *Recorder* that if he and his colleagues had met opposition

17. Article in *The Central Christian Advocate* reprinted in the *Christian Recorder*, October 6, 1866; December 1, 1866. The relationship of this church to the A.M.E. Church will be explored later in this chapter.
18. See the *Christian Recorder* for November 3, 1866; November 10, 1866; November 17, 1866.

from the M.E. Church, South they would not have been surprised. But to encounter such opposition from the M.E. Church, North astounded them. "What is it which prompts the agents of that church," he asked, "to tear down the work of colored men among colored men, the very people whom they profess to come to benefit?" In seeking the black people of the South, the A.M.E. Church was about its "legitimate business . . . organizing them into churches and schools." The black church had restricted its endeavors to Negroes and in no way interfered with the efforts of the M.E. Church, North and South to elevate southern whites. Desiring only to work with their own people, A.M.E. missionaries had "appealed to them, called them to become a happy and a God fearing people; to elevate themselves by industry, frugality, morality and religious improvement." The missionaries of the M.E. Church, North were the only "class of professing Christians" opposing the "noble work of the A.M.E. Church." Agents of the white church, Cain complained, were offering money to his subordinates "as an inducement for them to leave the A.M.E. Church and join the M.E. Church, North.[19]

His observations mark a turning point in A.M.E. missionary strategy. By 1866 it was apparent to the hierarchy of the black church that they could not expect to receive any help from the M.E. Church, North. It was also obvious that a union with their competitors would mean the end of the mission of the A.M.E. Church. To prevent a takeover and to achieve their goal of Negro uplift, the black churchmen effected a temporary understanding with the M.E. Church, South.

This tactic incensed the hierarchy of the M.E. Church, North. One of its missionaries serving in Mississippi wrote to his superiors that "the African . . . Church endorses every slander breathed against the M.E. Church and its functionaries . . . by the M.E. Church, South." The northern Methodists believed that nothing good could come of this alliance. A.M.E. missionaries in the South, they charged, had "fallen into the hands of unscrupulous adepts in ecclesiastical strategy, who [were] using them for most unworthy ends." If the northern wing of the A.M.E. Church did not control its representatives in the South, the M.E. Church, North charged, they would find themselves irreversibly linked to a church which had been "false to Civil and religious liberty." Moreover, in pursuing this policy A.M.E. missionaries were allying themselves with the "relentless

19. *Christian Recorder*, May 19, 1866.

foes of [their] people" and turning against the "very measures, which under *Divine* Providence, secured to the colored people the boon of emancipation." In short, the A.M.E. Church was being false to both God and
country.[20]

The black churchmen responded to these charges by calling their ac-
cusers racist. They also charged them with the equally serious crime of
being in "opposition to history," or Divine Providence. Since its formation
in 1816, the members and hierarchy of the A.M.E. Church had thought of
themselves as an instrument of God's will. God, they believed, had enjoined them to "build up a grand Negro organization which might be
[His] instrument in redeeming the Negro everywhere in general, and Africa in particular." To these black Christians the missionary aims of the
M.E. Church, North represented a thwarting of the Divine Will. The
M.E. Church, North's "love of aggrandizement leads her to turn streams
of water into her channel that God never designed to flow there. She pre-
vents the colored Methodist openly and by intrigue from becoming a
unit, and thus putting themselves in positions to do work which God as-
signs them by echoes of two voices, history and providence." Beneath this
religious rhetoric, then, lay the omnipresent task of Negro uplift, a goal
that could not be delegated to white Methodists because it would lead to
racial apostasy. They would turn the black Methodists of America away
from their historic mission and the impulse to elevate blacks throughout
the world would be lost in a solipsistic Americanism.

This sense of mission prompted the hierarchs of the A.M.E. Church to
become allies of the M.E. Church, South. Wishing to inherit the property
and black members of that church, A.M.E. missionaries joined forces with
their former enemies. Another factor contributing to this alliance was the
awareness of A.M.E. missionaries that once the struggle for souls was
over they would have to live with the dominant Methodism of the section. Thus, when the M.E. Church, North accused the black church of
treason, it seriously misread its rival's motives.[21]

2   According to a census taken in 1860–1861, the M.E. Church, South
had over 200,000 black members. This figure was to be drastically re-

20. Quoted in Morrow, *Northern Methodism and Reconstruction*, 137; *New Orleans Ad-
    vocate*, quoted in *Christian Recorder*, March 2, 1867.
21. *Christian Recorder*, April 21, 1866; August 22, 1868.

duced by 1866 because of the missionary efforts of the M.E. Church, North, the A.M.E. Church, and A.M.E. Zion Church in the urban and rural areas of the South. Capitalizing on disturbed conditions in the South and on a desire of the ex-slaves to test their new freedom, the northern churches organized defectors from the southern church into congregations. After five years of war the southern church's organizational structures were in disarray and "submerged" as one observer described it, "in the general wreck of the South." Despite the chaotic condition in which it found itself, the southern church did to some extent resist its northern predators by playing the northern churches off against one another.[22]

Initially, the southern church's animosity was directed toward the M.E. Church, North. Northern Methodist ministers who attempted to assume the pulpits of some southern churches were greeted with hostility by their rebel parishioners. Viewing the northern church as an agent of Republicanism, a few ministers of the M.E. Church, South urged their black congregations to join either the A.M.E. or A.M.E. Zion churches. They thought it would be better to have the blacks unite with the Negro organizations than to strengthen their old enemy. One minister of the southern church wrote to James Lynch and asked him to send copies of the *Recorder* and books to show to his congregation. He also urged Lynch to send an A.M.E. missionary to "organize [the] colored people of his congregation." In Charleston the M.E. Church, South allowed the A.M.E. Church to use three of its buildings while the A.M.E. Emanuel Church was under construction. A similar courtesy was extended to the black Methodists of Raymond, Mississippi, by the white Methodists of that town.[23]

However, it would be a mistake to conclude from these examples of Christian fellowship that all southern Methodists cooperated with the A.M.E. Church. The alliance was actually rather fragile. Some churches refused to turn over to the A.M.E. Church properties they held for their black members. Their intransigent behavior led James Lynch to declare that whatever right the white people had to these buildings "was a right

22. Morrow, *Northern Methodism and Reconstruction*, 129; Sweet, "Methodist Church Influence in Southern Politics"; quoted in Hunter D. Farish, *The Circuit Rider Dismounts: A Social History of Southern Methodism, 1865–1900* (Richmond: Dietz Press, 1938), 27.
23. Morrow, *Northern Methodism and Reconstruction*, 97–99, 133; Sweet, "The Methodist Episcopal Church and Reconstruction," 159; *Christian Recorder*, June 16, 1866;

de jure," which he claimed "had been impaired by the destruction of the civil government"; on the other hand, the colored people "had a right de facto," which was unimpaired and would be acknowledged by military authority. His arguments did not persuade the southern Methodists to change their minds. Hiram Revels, who served as an A.M.E. missionary in Vicksburg, Mississippi, before he was elected to the United States Senate, wrote to the *Recorder* to report that his congregation had been turned out of their building by the southern Methodists. A few months later an A.M.E. congregation in Natchez suffered a similar fate.[24]

The black churches didn't always finish second in these skirmishes over property, preachers, and members. In Charleston, for example, when the southern Methodists tried to reassert their control over the black Methodist churches of that city, the communicants refused to listen to the ministers who were assigned them. Such resistance reached a peak in Georgia, where the General Conference of the M.E. Church, South sent ministers to "all the colored churches." Several of these congregations refused to hear their ministers designate, and in Marietta, Georgia, the white minister was voted out while he was in the pulpit.[25]

Either the black churchmen were unaware that the alliance with the M.E. Church, South was tenuous or were so heartened by the kindness proferred by the southern Methodist, that they did not realistically assess their position in the struggle for black souls. Later events suggest that the A.M.E. Church was being used by the M.E. Church, South to frustrate the ambitions of its northern rival. The buildings and members it turned over to the A.M.E. Church may have been holdings that were about to be seized by the northern Methodists. The southern Church clearly opted for a lesser evil. Dazzled by what appeared to be expressions of good will, the clergy and members of the A.M.E. Church praised their new-found friends. These encomiums were not completely unwarranted. Some ministers of the M.E. Church, South did want the blacks affiliated with their church to unite with the A.M.E. Church. One of them told his congregation after they had united with the black church that "the redemption

T. Holt, *The Emergence of Negro Political Leadership in South Carolina During Reconstruction* (Ph.D. dissertation, Yale University, 1973), 149–50; *Christian Recorder*, May 11, 1867.

24. *Christian Recorder*, February 4, 1865; October 21, 1865; October 7, 1865; December 2, 1865.

25. *Christian Recorder*, October 21, 1865; December 30, 1865.

and elevation of the colored race was to a greater extent than ever before placed in [their] hands."[26]

Henry M. Turner, after speaking with two ministers of the M.E. Church, South in Georgia, reported to the *Recorder* that they had endorsed the work of the A.M.E. Church. These ministers, he claimed, had assured him that the black church "would never have any trouble about church property . . . [and] that it was the universal desire of their preachers and bishops to have all of their colored members unite with the A.M.E. Church." The assurances seem to have disarmed Turner. He did not ask the white men about the efforts their church had made during the preceding year to appoint ministers to the black Methodist churches in Georgia. Nor did he remind the ministers of other examples of M.E. Church, South perfidy. The black missionaries' reticence was part of a public relations campaign orchestrated by the hierarchy of the A.M.E. Church to dispel any reservations the southerners might have about their northern black coreligionists.[27]

The high point in this crusade to win friends and influence old enemies came in New Orleans in the spring of 1866, when the A.M.E. Church dispatched delegates to the General Conference of the M.E. Church, South. Five years of war had left the southern church in a sad state. Its circuits, stations, and conferences were in disarray and barely functioning. The A.M.E. Church concluded that the southern church would either disappear or be absorbed by its northern rival. If this happened, the African ecclesiastics asked themselves, what was to become of their brothers who were affiliated with the rebel church? Since the black churchmen were not prepared to let this rich prize fall into the hands of the M.E. Church, North the A.M.E. sent envoys to the New Orleans meeting who were instructed to request the transfer of the southern church's black members and their property. When the A.M.E. officials arrived at the conference, they were treated rather shabbily. Their presence and the existence of the A.M.E. Church was acknowledged, but the black men were not introduced to the assembled General Conference. Although they had been insulted, the African clerics did not withdraw but stayed and saw the conference reject their church's petition.[28]

26. *Christian Recorder*, December 21, 1865; May 19, 1866; June 16, 1866; December 21, 1865.
27. *Christian Recorder*, June 16, 1866; December 30, 1865; May 12, 1866; June 2, 1866.
28. *Christian Recorder*, April 21, 1866; May 19, 1866.

In rejecting the A.M.E. request, the M.E. Church, South announced to the other religious organizations eager to acquire its black members that it would take care of them. A committee established by the church to deal with the question of Negro membership reported to the conference that it had considered working out an alliance with the A.M.E. Church but because the M.E. Church, South had reservations, the union had not been consummated. By the late 1860s there was a growing suspicion in the minds of southerners that the A.M.E. Church was politicizing the freedmen. Thinking then that A.M.E. ministers would corrupt their black members, the M.E. Church, South refused to let them become a part of the black church.

To keep its black members, the M.E. Church, South offered them two plans of association. Those black people who wished to maintain a close relationship with the M.E. Church, South were permitted to worship under what was called the "old order." That is, they could continue to worship either with whites or in separate all-black congregations, as they had done before the war. Blacks who opted for the latter choice could choose their own ministers, who did not have to be white. Churches operating under these prewar guidelines were an integral part of the M.E. Church, South's conference system. Blacks who accepted the "old order" were to have no voice in church affairs; their status remained unchanged in the M.E. Church, South. Realizing that some of its Negro members might find these conditions distasteful, the southern church offered to organize these people into separate congregations, districts, and conferences. It also promised to ordain ministers and appoint presiding elders who would direct the affairs of this consocation of churches.

The independence granted blacks under the "new law" was more illusory than real. The M.E. Church, South still owned the buildings in which the Negroes worshiped, and through its power of ordination it determined who was to preach for them and run their affairs as presiding elder. In establishing this conference, then, the M.E. Church, South had given up very little. What it had done, though, was prevent the majority of its black members from joining the A.M.E. Church. The southern church's decision, when viewed in this context, appears to have been a holding action. Its black members had been given time to develop their own leaders and concurrently decide what they wanted to do. When the General Conference of the M.E. Church, South convened in Memphis in

1870, the delegates were informed that the Negroes had formed five annual conferences and wanted to establish a church of their own. The conference accepted this decision and offered to ordain the men the blacks
selected as their bishops. Thus in 1870 was born the Colored Methodist
Episcopal Church. It received as a parting gift from the M.E. Church,
South all the property that the A.M.E. Church wanted to acquire.[29]

If the A.M.E. Church detested its white rival, it abominated the black
one, the African Methodist Episcopal Zion Church. This animus dated
back to the late eighteenth century, when both churches emerged as off-
shoots of the Methodist Church. The A.M.E. Zion Church traces its origins back to 1796, when the blacks who worshiped in the John Street
Methodist Church of New York City withdrew because they were segregated as Richard Allen and his followers had been in Philadelphia. From
1800 to 1819 the Zionites existed as an independent congregation within
the Methodist Church. During this time the Methodist supplied the black
congregation with preachers. Ultimately the arrangement proved to be
unworkable because the blacks began to resent the control the whites exercised over their affairs. Casting about for alternatives, the Zionites asked
Bishop Allen of the A.M.E. Church to ordain a minister for them. He
agreed, so that they could have a resident minister. The man chosen by the
New Yorkers to become their pastor was William Lambert. He was dispatched to Philadelphia but when he returned to New York he stunned the
Zionites by establishing a new church rather than serving them. Suspicious
of Bishop Allen, the Zionites believed that he had encouraged Lambert to
desert them and that he was only interested in building up the A.M.E.
Church. This suspicion was correct. Bishop Allen did indeed want to unite
all black Methodists into one church, but he often alienated other blacks
because of his aggressive and domineering behavior.[30]

The Lambert affair did not end the Zionites' contacts with the A.M.E.

29. For the origins of the C.M.E. Church, see the *Nashville Christian Advocate* reprinted in
the *Christian Recorder*, September 8, 1866; see also the article reprinted from the *Advocate* in the *Christian Recorder*, on October 6, 1866; Crum, *The Negro in the Methodist Church*, 55; Farish, *The Circuit Rider Dismounts*, 170; Hartzell, "Methodism
and the Negro in the United States," 311; C. H. Phillips, *The History of the C.M.E.
Church in America* (Jackson, Tenn.: C.M.E. Church, 1898), 22–23.
30. For the origins of this church see Crum, *The Negro in the Methodist Church*, 20; Christopher Rush, *Rise and Progress of the African Methodist Episcopal Church* (New York:
Christopher Rush, 1843); Payne, *History of The African Methodist Episcopal Church*,
34–36.

bishop. However, in 1820, when he asked them to become a part of his flock, they refused, fearing a loss of their independence. Since the congregation still lacked an ordained minister, they asked the white minister who had led them out of the Methodist Church to ordain their leaders. He agreed, and Zionite independence was thus assured.[31]

Although the church the Zionites established in 1821 was incorporated as the African Methodist Episcopal Church, its title was a misnomer. The new church differed radically from other Methodist churches because it was not an Episcopal Church. In the A.M.E. Zion Church the presiding officers were superintendents and not bishops as they were in other Methodist churches. At first the superintendents were elected yearly and supervised only the preachers, quarterly conferences, and churches of the connection. In 1824 their term of office was extended to four years, and they were allowed to supervise the annual conferences of the church. The church was administered by superintendents until 1868, when its Annual Conference voted to abolish the office and have bishops. The change may have been a response to A.M.E. charges that the Zion Church was an illegitimate member of the Methodist family.[32]

The antipathy that the A.M.E. Church displayed toward the A.M.E. Zion Church both before and after the Civil War resulted from frustration. Believing themselves to be the agents of God's providence, the bishops of the A.M.E. Church wanted to unite all the black Methodists in America under their banner. They never achieved this goal because the Zionites refused to unite with them. The Zion Church was not so large as its rival; before the war the church's growth had been hampered by internal struggles. The Zionites were, nevertheless, able to develop an *esprit de corps* which made them distinct from the A.M.E. Church. In refusing the A.M.E. Church's offer of union, the Zionites were preserving their sense of self. Although they were not trying to be either intransigent or capricious, they enraged the A.M.E. Church, which moved quickly to block the southward expansion of its black competitor.[33]

31. Wesley, *Richard Allen: Apostle of Freedom*, 178–79; Crum, *The Negro in the Methodist Church*, 20; Rush, *Rise and Progress of the African Methodist Episcopal Church*, 66–67; Bucke, *The History of American Methodism*, II, 563.

32. Bucke, *The History of American Methodism*, II, 563–66; *Christian Recorder*, May 19, 1866; June 16, 1866; see also the article reprinted from *Zions Standard* in *Christian Recorder*, September 22, 1866; June 16, 1866.

33. In 1848 the church added the word *Zion* to its title to differentiate it from the A.M.E.

The ensuing struggle between the two churches resembled the A.M.E.'s fights with the M.E. Church, North. Indeed, when viewed in a broader perspective, this conflict was nothing more than another front in an interdenominational war. Although one A.M.E. missionary declared that the strife was "a sin before God," his colleagues do not seem to have been bothered by such considerations. To them, the A.M.E. Zion Church was an enemy to be destroyed or discredited. They told the freedmen who were members of the M.E. Church, South that they could not join the A.M.E. Zion without repudiating their belief in episcopacy. This argument was a strong one because many of the freedmen who called themselves Methodist probably could not conceive of being members of a church without bishops. The office held certain historical associations for them which differentiated their church from the Baptist and Presbyterian. The possibility that joining the A.M.E. Zion Church would somehow compromise their faith may have dissuaded those blacks who were thinking about becoming Zionites. Several months after these charges were made, some Zionites recommended that the Annual Conference of their church convene in special session for "the purpose of choosing, electing, and having ordained or ordaining bishops." This step, they claimed, would move them in the direction of union with the Methodist churches, which were governed by bishops. What is not clear, though, is whether the request was directly related to the A.M.E. Church's accusations.[34]

The lack of an episcopacy did not weaken the Zionites' resolve to win converts among the freedmen. Missionaries of the A.M.E. Zion Church reciprocated the A.M.E. Church's hostility. In Louisville, for example, a Zionite minister told the members of the Center Street Church that the Discipline of the A.M.E. Church supported slavery. He then questioned the validity of the A.M.E. Church's episcopacy. The Episcopal bishop who had ordained Richard Allen, the A.M.E. Zion minister declared, was not connected with any church when he officiated at the ordination.

Church. After the Civil War several attempts were made to unite the A.M.E. and A.M.E. Zion Churches. These efforts were not successful because the two churches continued to view each other with suspicion. For the problem of union before the war see George, *Segregated Sabbaths*, 99–101; for the post–Civil War period see Bishop William J. Walls, *The African Methodist Episcopal Zion Church* (Charlotte: A.M.E. Zion Publishing House, 1974), 460–74.

34. *Christian Recorder*, May 13, 1865; May 19, 1866; June 16, 1866; see the article reprinted from *Zions Standard* in *Christian Recorder*, June 16, 1866; September 22, 1866.

Similar attempts by the A.M.E. ministers to discredit the A.M.E. Zion Church suggest that the tactic was a successful means to win converts either way.

But in the struggle to acquire new members, the Zionites did more than emulate their adversaries. Taking the offensive, they put A.M.E. missionaries on the defensive and forced them to defend their church, its policies, and their own reputations. Henry Turner wrote to the *Recorder* that he had to respond to the following calumnies: "that I was a Bethelite, and did not believe in hell; that I believed Jesus Christ was a mere man; and another report, which was that I was a Campbellite whose doctrine was that women have no souls, and that the devil would one day break his chain and get loose." Upset by these accusations and by the fact that some of the freedmen were beginning to believe them, Turner took two days to refute the charges. A.M.E. missionaries serving in various locales, Turner reported to the paper, were being told by the freedmen, "You can't get into our pulpit." Taking advantage of the freedmen's credulity, one A.M.E. Zion missionary told a group of ex-slaves in Augusta, Georgia, that the A.M.E. Church was not known outside the state. The church, he said, was "a mere creation of Turner and Lynch, no such church being known in the North." This exercise in vilification concluded with the Zionite minister calling the A.M.E. clergy a collection of "barking dogs."[35]

These *ad hominem* attacks enabled the A.M.E. Zion Church to acquire new members and establish itself in the South. But looking to the future, A.M.E. Zion missionaries realized that character assassination and misrepresentation of their enemies' motives could be self-defeating. In a struggle in which all the participants claimed to be Christians, this un-Christlike behavior was a weak rock on which to erect a church. Therefore, to consolidate their church's position in the South, the Annual Conference of the A.M.E. Zion Church in 1867 "extended the right hand of fellowship" to the M.E. Church, South. Although this move provided the church with a friend, it also added another twist to the northern quest for southern black souls. It put the M.E. Church, South in the position of having to decide which of the two black churches was to inherit its

35. *Christian Recorder*, February 25, 1865; March 17, 1866; August 17, 1867; September 21, 1867; October 19, 1867.

Negro members and their property. The problem was resolved in 1870, when the southerners allowed their black members to organize the C.M.E. Church.[36]

The creation of this new church did not signal the end of hostilities between the A.M.E. and the A.M.E. Zion Churches. They continued to harass each other after 1870. Zionite missionaries apparently intensified their assault on the character and doctrine of the A.M.E. Church, for the General Conferences of the A.M.E. Church in 1872 created the office of state missionaries to counter Zionite propaganda. Every annual conference of the church was empowered to appoint one or two missionaries who were to tour the states where the church decided "to organize churches and missionary societies, and to inform the people of the origin, character, doctrine and progress of [the A.M.E.] Church." Just how effective this counterattack was is difficult to say. But the fact that the A.M.E. Church thought it was necessary to create the new office suggests that it felt threatened by the aspersions cast on its character.[37]

3   The decision of the M.E. Church, South in 1870 to permit its black members to organize a new church disappointed all the northern Methodist churches. Enraged, they turned against the C.M.E. Church. Effecting an informal alliance, the M.E. Church, North, A.M.E., and A.M.E. Zion Churches stigmatized the new organization by calling it "the rebel church," or "Democratic Church," or "the old slavery church," all epithets intended to discredit it in the eyes of the freedmen. It was depicted as a tool of the slavocrats: "The Colored Methodist Episcopal Church of America, South or of South America, or whatever it may be called, has the rickets, spinal complaint, and consumption. Instead of Gospel milk and meat, it has been fed upon Confederate politics, hatred to Yankees and official vanity till the poor thing is too dyspeptic to digest wholesome food. . . . Poor thing! It is a fit place for nobody but such as prefer to be in slavery and ignorance than free and educated."[38]

36. *Loyal Georgian*, July 6, 1867.
37. *Journal of the Fifteenth Quadrennial Session of the General Conference of the A.M.E. Church, Nashville, Tennessee*, May 6, 1872, p. 119.
38. Sweet, "The Methodist Episcopal Church and Reconstruction," 417; Phillips, *The History of the C.M.E. Church in America*, 71–72; Morrow, *Northern Methodism and Reconstruction*, 138–39; quoted in Farish, *The Circuit Rider Dismounts*, 173.

Such attacks influenced a number of freedmen to turn against the C.M.E. Church. Perceiving it to be a tool of the slaveholders, they refused to associate with those blacks who joined. Social ostracism was only one part of a general assault on the integrity of the new church. Abuse was both verbal and physical. In Thomasville, Georgia, for example, the C.M.E. Church was burned down and had to be rebuilt. A church in Tallahassee, Florida, which was destroyed by fire, was described as having been "in the furnace of affliction."[39]

The most serious malefactor in this campaign to destroy the C.M.E. Church was the A.M.E. Church. According to one bishop of the A.M.E. Church, "there was no need" for the C.M.E. Church. It served no useful purpose because the A.M.E. Church "was well organized" and could have taken care of the black Methodists of the South. The C.M.E. Church, Bishop Gaines declared, had been organized because the M.E. Church, South "feared the political influence of the North." The white southerners, he said, thought that the A.M.E. Church "was a political church in sympathy with the North." They were wrong. Although the A.M.E. Church "believed fully in the freedom of the race and appreciated those who brought about that freedom," it was not and never had been a "political church." The same thing could not be said, though, of the C.M.E. Church. Bishop Gaines and his colleagues believed that politics was the *raison d'etre* of the C.M.E. Church. The new church, they thought, was not dedicated, as the A.M.E. Church was, to the task of racial uplift. It was a product of southern chicanery and had been organized to frustrate the A.M.E. Church's grand design.[40]

To say, then, that the A.M.E. Church perceived the C.M.E. Church as an enemy would be an understatement. The hierarchy and members of the northern church thought that southern blacks who joined the C.M.E. Church were traitors to their race. This belief induced the A.M.E. Church to reject C.M.E. attempts to resolve the difficulties that existed between the two churches.

The major obstacle to a rapprochement was a dispute in 1870 over

39. Phillips, *The History of The C.M.E. Church in America,* 71–72; for a defense of this church see *The American Union,* April 2, 1869. For other discussions of this problem see *The American Union,* April 2, 1869; April 16, 1869; and August 27, 1869; Phillips, *The History of the C.M.E. Church in America,* 73–74.
40. Quoted in Gaines, *African Methodism in the South or Twenty-Five Years of Freedom,* 21–22.

property. During the course of its southern expansion, the A.M.E. Church acquired a number of buildings that were used by the black members of the M.E. Church, South. Although the edifices were registered as the property of the southern church, they had been paid for by the blacks who worshiped in them. When the M.E. Church, South emancipated its black members, it gave them the titles to these properties, and a struggle between the two black churches followed. The A.M.E. Church refused to give up the property which the C.M.E. Church claimed. To resolve the problem, the bishops of the C.M.E. Church dispatched a letter in 1872 to the General Conference of the A.M.E. Church which requested that the body appoint a committee to meet with them "to settle the dispute that now exists between our churches with regard to our church property that you are now occupying." The bishops went on to say that they did not want to sue to recover what was lawfully theirs, a threat by implication that they would sue if the A.M.E. Church ignored their request. When the letter was read to the General Conference of the A.M.E. Church, it was referred to a committee. The committee took a year to draft its reply, which turned out to be a masterful exercise in noncompliance. "Touching the question of property," the committee replied, "We are willing to act strictly according to the principle of equity and right, and earnestly hope that all disputes regarding the same may be amicably adjusted." But a solution based on these principles was not possible as long as the A.M.E. Church refused to accept the existence of the C.M.E. Church. It continued to believe that southern black Methodists were misguided in creating their own church, and that if they had understood the history, rise, and progress of the A.M.E. Church, the C.M.E. Church would not have been organized. This belief was a chimera that blinded the church to certain realities.[41]

Swollen with pride, the A.M.E. Church refused to grant to southern black Methodists a privilege it had claimed for itself since 1792—that is, the right of self-determination. If the C.M.E. Church represented anything, it was the desire of the southern blacks who joined it to control their religious life. For over two centuries this facet of their lives had been shaped by other people. Emancipation enabled the ex-slaves to establish

41. *Journal of Fifteenth Quadrennial Session of the General Conference of the A.M.E. Church*, May 6, 1872, Nashville, Tennessee, 25–26; quoted in Phillips, *The History of the C.M.E. Church in America*, 65–67.

their own churches and to worship as they pleased. To a number of the
freedmen the A.M.E. Church represented a threat to this process. "A very
large majority of the colored people desire something different from the
A.M.E. Church in its practices and objects, and we now give you our reason for saying so: There are large numbers of men going through the
country calling themselves ministers of the A.M.E. Church, whose sole
object is to secure money to build up that iniquitous publishing house in
Philadelphia, that does not and never will benefit us or our children." The
charge that the A.M.E. ministers were only interested in collecting money
to build up the northern branch of their church was repeated at a later
date by members of the Virginia Conference of the A.M.E. Church. The
accusation was hotly denied by Bishop Campbell, who was at the meeting. He told the assembled delegates that the "A.M.E. Church recognizes
no North, South, no East, no West in her legislation."[42]

To men like Bishop Campbell and other A.M.E. missionaries who
worked to establish the church in the South, these criticisms must have
seemed the rankest form of ingratitude. They had come South not to take
advantage of the freedmen but to elevate them. In pursuit of this goal,
they had encountered opposition from other Methodists and even from
Catholics. But throughout these travails they were sustained by the belief
that what they were doing was sanctioned by God and that His commission had been granted only to them.[43]

Believing this, they became suspicious of the efforts of other religious
organizations who tried to work with the freedmen. Their suspicions eventually poisoned even the church's relationship with the American Missionary Association, an unfortunate occurrence because the A.M.A. had
provided the church with money to finance its missionary endeavors when
other religious organizations refused. The fact that the A.M.A. helped
them when they were friendless was conveniently forgotten by the black
clerics in the 1870s, when they began to view their ally as an enemy. Officials of the church became upset with the A.M.A. because it retained the
title to buildings it erected in the South for the freedmen's use. The black
churchmen thought that the deed to these structures should be turned

42. *The American Union*, April 15, 1869; *Minutes of the Eighth Annual Session of the Virginia Conference of the A.M.E. Church, April 15, 1874, Danville, Virginia*, 34.
43. For A.M.E. opposition to Catholicism see *Christian Recorder*, October 27, 1866; and
the Report on Catholicism presented to *The Sixteenth Session and the Fifteenth Quadrennial Session of the General Conferences of the A.M.E. Church, May 1st, to 18th,
1876, Atlanta, Georgia*, 121–27.

over to the local communities. In making this claim, the A.M.E. Church was being disingenuous, because what it wanted was control of these buildings for its own use.[44]

In its expansion southward, then, the A.M.E. Church became a victim of its own rhetoric. Black churchmen were naive to think that they and they alone could uplift the freedmen. Their church lacked the resources to perform the task, and even if it had received financial support from other churches, it probably could not have accomplished its projected goal. But oblivious to the realities and believing themselves to be agents of God, A.M.E. missionaries persisted in their quest. As instruments of providence they pursued their task with a single-mindedness which bordered on the fanatic. This sense of commitment reflected their belief that the black race was in need of moral tutelage throughout the world. The church's mission to the slaves, then, was only the first step in a worldwide campaign to spread the benefit of American civilization to a benighted people. When the A.M.E. Church's missionary impulse is viewed from this perspective it loses some of its grandeur and becomes nothing more than another exercise in cultural homogenization. Like certain elements in the Anglo-Saxon population, these Afro-Saxons feared diversity and assumed that their way was best. This presumption helps to explain the church's hostility to other religious organizations who tried to work with the freedmen and its animus toward blacks who joined either the A.M.E. Zion, or C.M.E. Churches.[45]

44. For the A.M.E. Church's relations with the American Missionary Association, see Clara De Boer, "The Role of Afro-Americans in the Origin and Work of the American Missionary Association" (Ph.D. dissertation, Rutgers University, 1973). See also the letter from Lewis Tappan to Bishop Payne, January 31, 1868, in American Missionary Association Papers, Amistad Research Center, Dillard University. This letter suggests that the A.M.E. and A.M.A. also disagreed over working with the Unitarian Universalists. The A.M.A. did not consider the Universalists Christians. Just where the A.M.E. stood on this point is unclear.
45. *Christian Recorder*, November 21, 1868.

V Between the Buzzard and the Hawk: A.M.E. Ministers and the Politics of Reconstruction

The Civil War destroyed the institution of Negro slavery, but it did not eradicate the attitudes, values, and prejudices which were an integral part of the peculiar institution's *raison d'etre*. As leaders of the black community, A.M.E. ministers worked to change these perceptions and build a racially harmonious South in which men would have equal opportunity regardless of their color. In assuming this task they were alternately sanguine and pessimistic. Although the ministers believed that the war would result in the emancipation of their people, freedom, they realized, would present the ex-slaves with a new set of problems. As a consequence a number of A.M.E. ministers entered the tangled web of Reconstruction politics.[1]

When asked why he had become a politician, Charles Pearce replied: "A man in this state cannot do his whole duty as a minister except he looks out for the political interests of his people. They are like ships out at sea, and they must have somebody to guide them; and it is natural that they should get their best informed men to lead them." Whether the A.M.E. ministers were the "best informed men" is debatable. What is not contestable is the fact that they became involved in the rough and tumble of post–Civil War politics only to learn "that revolutions . . . do go backwards." Their vision of a new and egalitarian South rising from the ashes of war never became a reality. The black clergymen's failure to achieve

1. For this duality in A.M.E. thought, see the *Christian Recorder* for July 20, 1861; September 7, 1861; June 14, 1862; December 6, 1862; January 10, 1863; July 18, 1863; April 23, 1864; May 7, 1864; June 11, 1864; May 27, 1865; June 17, 1865; April 21, 1866; Charleston *Daily Courier*, May 19, 1865.

this goal should not be attributed to a lack of "political consciousness" or to a lack of will. Rather it should be seen as a product of forces beyond their control, forces which one black politician recognized when he said, "Negroes, as a race, are between the hawk of Republican demagogism and the buzzard of Democratic prejudices."[2]

1   In its advance southward the A.M.E. Church encountered opposition from both black and white southerners. Most southern blacks rejected the church's ministrations because they wanted to establish a religious life of their own. They also feared the cultural dominance of their northern brothers and wanted ministers who respected their folk ways. These differences, though, did not make them, in most instances, hostile to the A.M.E. Church's political activities. This was not the case with southern whites, the majority of whom believed that the black church would disrupt their communities. To them the A.M.E. Church was an agent of Republicanism, and they thought it would instill notions of equality in the freedmen. Since the A.M.E. Church sought to elevate the ex-slaves, such fears were not unwarranted. Once the former bondsmen became educated and self-reliant, the A.M.E. hierarchy believed, the old patterns of deference would disappear and blacks and whites would meet as equals. This possibility frightened southern whites and made the work of the A.M.E. Church difficult.[3]

To mollify the fears of southerners, the church denied that it "was a political church in sympathy with the north." This disclaimer was rather disingenuous. The A.M.E. Church was not a political organization, but its sympathies were with the North. That is to say, it wanted northern arms to triumph in the conflict and the slaves freed. To achieve these ends, the church, after some hesitancy, encouraged its members and other free blacks to enlist in the Union cause. It also leased buildings to the

2.   *Testimony Taken by the Joint Select Committee to Inquire into the Condition of Affairs in the Late Insurrectionary States* (13 vols.; Washington: Government Printing Office, 1872), XIII, 171. See also R. H. Cain's remarks in the Atlanta *Constitution*, November 28, 1868; *Christian Recorder*, May 7, 1864; Eugene D. Genovese, "Legacy of Slavery and Roots of Black Nationalism," *Studies on the Left*, VI (1967), 14; *Semi-Weekly Louisianian*, August 3, 1871.
3.   *Minutes of the Pittsburgh Annual Conference of the A.M.E. Church, held in Brownsville, Pennsylvania, April 15–20, 1871* (Pittsburgh: W. S. Haven & Co., 1871). See also Smith, *A History of the African Methodist Episcopal Church*, 520.

Union army for hospitals when others were not available. These actions constituted direct contributions to the northern war effort and hardly suggest that the church was neutral·in the conflict. If, during the hostilities, any A.M.E. literature had fallen into rebel hands, it would not have been difficult to discern where the church's sympathy lay. When President Lincoln issued his Preliminary Proclamation of Emancipation in 1862, for example, the Ohio Conference of the A.M.E. Church adopted a report which hailed "with infinite delight this act by which the manacles have been struck from the limbs of thousands of our brothers and sisters." Nevertheless, the A.M.E. Church's endorsement of the federal government's policies was not unqualified. As the Reconstruction process unfolded, that fact became even clearer.[4]

To the members and hierarchy of the A.M.E. Church, the Civil War was a moral conflict between slavery and liberty, a struggle for the rights of man which would culminate in the realization of the ideas embodied in the Declaration of Independence. The catalyst for this change, the black churchmen believed, was the Republican party. Their expectations for the party were extremely high. Daniel Alexander Payne, a bishop of the church, made this point when he told a group of black men in Washington: "Our votes, our prayers aided in securing the success of that party. It is not enough that it has success; it must have love—a love for humanity stronger than its love for race—a love for justice stronger than its love for power. Liberty, justice, love must triumph in that party, and over that party, leaving it completely captive."[5]

The Republican party never lived up to the bishop's expectations. He thought, as other members of his church did, that the party was ready to

---

4. Gaines, *African Methodism in the South or Twenty-Five Years of Freedom*, 21–22; *Christian Recorder*, September 7, 1861; *Minutes of the Thirty-second Session of the Ohio Annual Conference of the A.M.E. Church, Held in Zanesville City, Ohio, from April 15 to 23, 1862* (Zanesville, Ohio: Printed at the *Daily Courier* Office, 1862). See the church's endorsement of Republicans in *Christian Recorder*, November 1867; March 20, 1869. See also the endorsement for James Lynch in the *Christian Recorder*, October 30, 1869.

5. See Bishop Payne's letter to "The National Convention of Colored Citizens of the United States, at Washington Assembled," printed in *Proceedings of the National Convention of the Colored Men of America, Held in Washington, D.C. on January 13, 14, 15, and 16, 1869* (Washington, D.C.: Great Republican Book and Newspaper Printing Establishment, 1869), 15. See also Payne's Sermon, *The Moral Significance of the 15th Amendment* (Xenia: Printed by the Xenia Gazette Co., 1870), 4, 5, 6, for some other laudatory comments about the Republicans.

afford complete equality to Negroes. In thinking this, however, the black churchmen profoundly misread Republican intentions and the extent to which the party shared the prevailing racial prejudices. What the ecclesiasts failed to see was that the party was not unified on the question of race or Negro rights. If there was a mainstream position among Republicans on this subject, it was that Negroes were human and therefore entitled to the rights of life, liberty, and property. Most Republicans were unwilling to go beyond these minimal civil guarantees. They did not believe that blacks should enjoy political or social equality with whites. The commitment to the Negro was hedged with qualifications, and in no way approximated the church's conception of what the Negroes' position should be in a reconstructed nation. These differences between the party and the church became apparent as the war entered its final year.[6]

The A.M.E. Church wanted civil and political equality for black people. It denied the charge that the granting of these rights would lead to interracial marriages. Black men and women, the church said, were only interested in marrying each other, "like their brethren and sisters of the white race." Those individuals who wanted to marry across racial lines would find it difficult to do so because of public hostilities. To further allay white fears that black enfranchisement would lead to miscegenation, the church cited the examples of the Jews. To nineteenth-century blacks, the Jews were the classic example of a people who had been able to succeed despite adversity. The relationship of Jews to American society, some churchmen thought, held important lessons for black people.

> They, [the Jews], enjoy all the privileges that any white American enjoys in this country. They have their oath in every state, hold office, fill the scientific and learned professions, meet at commercial boards. Yet there is not so much social commingling between the Jews and the white Americans as between the white Americans and the black man. Consider the proposition . . . that the guarantee of Civil and full political rights to the black man does not necessarily bring about a social commingling of white and black as a necessary result.

Without a vote, the church argued, the black man would be a cipher in a society which accorded this privilege to other free men. He would be stig-

---

6. Foner, *Free Soil, Free Labor, Free Men.* See his Chapter 8 for the Republican's silence on questions of social equality.

matized as an inferior breed of man whose rights other men did not have
to respect. In advocating that the Negro be enfranchised, the ministers
and members of the church were not entirely sanguine. R. H. Cain, one
of the church's most articulate young preachers, warned black people not
to be too optimistic about the future once the war was over. Although
there were people in the North who were willing to accord "the colored
man many of his rights," deep rooted prejudice still persisted and unscrupulous politicians sought to incite "low," "vulgar" "vagabonds" to "kill
the nigger." To Cain and his coreligionists, racial prejudice was "the Greatest Folly of white Americans." This character flaw, they argued, could not
be justified on any grounds; it was both irrational and hypocritical.[7]

White Americans, blacks argued, needed to change the criterion by
which they assessed other people's suitability for the franchise. Color was
a poor way to evaluate another man's worth. Color discrimination worked
to the detriment of the United States. An examination of the country's
immigration policies, one member of the church declared, would sub-
stantiate this observation. America had opened her doors to thousands of
foreigners and had given them social and economic preferment over the
Negro. But some of these people, he observed, were not good citizens.
This was particularly true of the Irish, whose behavior showed that they
did not appreciate their citizenship. Once invested with the franchise, the
Irish forgot their former life of hardship and began "to bully the government." Disregarding the law of the land, they "rioted, ransacked cities,"
"murdered colored children," "and burned down orphan asylums." Ignorant of American customs and traditions, foreigners were susceptible to
the blandishments of the enemies of freedom. If the slave power should
attempt to reassert itself, the government was going to need allies. Because the Negro was native-born and had from birth imbibed the principal tenets of Americanism, he was a more suitable candidate for enfranchisement than the thousands of aliens flocking to the country's shores.[8]

7. *Christian Recorder*, March 10, 1865; July 15, 1866. For A.M.E. idealization of the
   Jews, see Daniel Alexander Payne (ed.), *The Semi-Centenary and the Retrospection of
   The A.M.E. Church in the U.S.A.* (Baltimore: Sherwood & Co., 1866) 169. *Christian
   Recorder*, April 23, 1864; November 11, 1865. This article is interesting because
   the church saw in the North a combination of rich and poor whites opposed to black
   suffrage.
8. *Christian Recorder*, March 3, 1865; September 9, 1865; February 9, 1867; June 11,
   1864. For some other criticisms of the preferential treatment which foreigners received

Initially these criticisms were lost on people to whom they were addressed, since those did not feel threatened by the country's new citizens. As the war drew to a close, there was even a noticeable softening in the North's attitude toward the South. President Lincoln's second inaugural plea, for malice toward none and charity for all, touched a responsive chord in the Yankee psyche. Rapprochement between the two sections became even more of a possibility after Richmond fell and Lee surrendered. With the war over, many northerners were willing to forgive their former enemies. This mellowed mood toward the South, the A.M.E. Church feared, might be translated into a reconstruction policy which failed to secure the rights of Negroes. If the fate of southern blacks was to be decided by the legislatures of the states in which they resided, the church argued, Congress would be "opening a slaughter house for human flesh." Defeated in battle and hating the government, southerners would vent their frustrations on the emancipated slaves. Thinking that this was the course which the government was about to follow, the church became more vociferous after President Lincoln was assassinated and Andrew Johnson succeeded him as president.[9]

In evaluating the pleas for Negro enfranchisement made by the clergy and members of the church, it would be easy to argue that they were prescient and recognized that Johnson was not a friend of the Negro or of the North. This was not the case, at least not in April, 1865. The blacks seem to have been genuinely disturbed that the government, regardless of the president heading it, was about to exclude the Negro from the Reconstruction process. On May 13, 1865, for example, the *Christian Recorder* warned the North to be on its guard. The South's submission to northern arms, the *Recorder* said, did not mean that the rebels had abandoned the principles which had animated them before the war. If anything, these ideas were now even more dangerous to the nation. Before secession the South's treason had been overt—now it would be covert. It was the government's duty, therefore, to establish a "protective system" which encompassed more than arms. "The classes that stood united and firm on the battlefield, in the cause of union and liberty," both black and white,

over Negroes, see January 7, 1865; July 1, 1865. Why the Irish hated blacks is discussed in January 29, 1870; June 11, 1864. On the question of southern reassertion, see May 13, 1865.
9. McPherson, *The Struggle for Equality*, 309; *Christian Recorder*, March 10, 1865.

would now have to unite at the ballot box, to support the same cause. By voting together, still another A.M.E. spokesman noted, the loyal whites of the South and the enfranchised blacks were numerous enough to control the "old slave states" and insure their loyalty.[10]

To northern charges that "the mass of population in the South, both black and white, were ignorant," churchmen replied that this was also true of the majority of northern voters and that ultimately education was irrelevant as a determinant of patriotism. "Education is good," an A.M.E. member wrote, "but it appears that some of the staunchest patriots in the land cannot read; and that some of the basest traitors are highly educated. Education, although at the expense of their country, did not prevent Lee and his associates from trying to destroy their country. Robert Smalls, whether he can read or not, is to our thinking a much sounder and safer voter than Toombs." In urging the government to enfranchise the freedmen, the church did not forget the adverse conditions under which northern Negroes were forced to live. It asked the elected officials and people of the North to remove the barriers which prevented blacks from receiving "even-handed justice."[11]

Like the Republicans, most northerners were not committed to granting blacks complete social and political equality. At the same time, they did not believe that the freedmen should be re-enslaved. This ambiguity in northern thought about the Negroes' future position in American society encouraged President Johnson to initiate a Reconstruction program which alarmed both the North and the A.M.E. Church. President Johnson pursued policies which encouraged southerners to think that Reconstruction was going to be an executive function. Taking their cues from the president, the former rebels proceeded to behave in ways which gave credence to A.M.E. charges that the South was unregenerate. They formed state governments dominated by former Confederates who seemed to be oblivious to the changes which five years of internecine strife had wrought in the South. Ignoring the Thirteenth Amendment, they enacted "black codes" which prescribed for vagrancy and the violation of labor contracts punishments similar to those in the old slave codes. Emboldened by the president's laissez-faire attitude, southerners also began to use extralegal means to intimidate the freedmen.[12]

10. *Christian Recorder*, May 13, 1865; May 27, 1865.
11. *Christian Recorder*, May 27, 1865; June 10, 1865.
12. For an interesting discussion of how the South interpreted President Johnson's Recon-

Three months after Johnson became president, one member of the A.M.E. Church, living in Mississippi, wrote to the *Christian Recorder* that he had received a letter from Montgomery, Alabama, which informed him "that colored men [were] coming in from the interior of the state horribly mutilated. One having his ears cut off, and otherwise inhumanly bruised and hacked." He went on to say that conditions in Mississippi were equally bad. Reports from there told of "the colored people . . . being killed, their entrails cut out, and fiendishly outraged." Most of these atrocities, the A.M.E. correspondent said, occurred in the countryside where Union forces were weak and the blacks could not be protected effectively. But in the cities where the military was stronger, he continued, the freedmen did not seem to fare any better. In Natchez, for instance, they were subject to a variety of abuses.

> Colored people here are excessively taxed; for a pass or permit to work for six months, or less, they must pay three dollars or more. For every little script of writing they pay from one dollar to five, and sometimes even more. Men and women pay poll tax of two dollars. In many of the Freedmen's schools, each scholar pays from one twenty-five to two fifty per month. In many other shameful ways their ignorance and helplessness are taken advantage of, even to a forcible violation of the virtues of their wives and daughters by white guards and soldiers.

Responsibility for this sad state of affairs, he thought, lay with the government. To him, it seemed to be the policy of Union officials throughout the south "to fully reinstate the rebels into power" and abandon the freedmen to their maliciousness.[13]

After the summer of 1865, the laity and hierarchy of the church vigorously protested the Johnson plan of Reconstruction—a program which they believed rewarded the nation's enemies and punished its friends. In Congress, meanwhile, both the moderate and radical wings of the Republican party finally responded to southern intransigence. Between 1866–1867 the Republicans passed a series of laws which gave control of Reconstruction to Congress, protected freedmen from southern harassment, and gave blacks the vote. Coupled with a humanitarian con-

---

struction policy, see Eric McKitrick, *Andrew Johnson and Reconstruction* (Chicago, University of Chicago Press, 1960), 153–214.

13. *Christian Recorder*, July 1, 1865. See also *The Condition of Affairs in the Late Insurrectionary States*, XIII, 166.

cern for the Negro was an even more pressing desire to establish the party's hegemony over national affairs, and to consolidate its wartime gains. The issue of Negro rights enabled the party to accomplish these goals.[14]

2   The Reconstruction Act of 1867 provided Negroes with the opportunity to participate in southern politics. Taking advantage of this situation, a heterogeneous group of twenty-three A.M.E. Church missionaries became politicians. Only three were northerners, the rest from the South and the border states. Six of these men had been born free, one as a youth had been indentured, and the remaining sixteen were ex-slaves. All of the minister-politicians were educated, some having attended college, the others being either self-taught or the recipients of some form of schooling.[15]

This group of men included some of the brightest and most talented missionaries in the A.M.E. Church. Among them was T. W. Stringer of Vicksburg, who before he came South worked as an A.M.E. missionary in Ohio and Canada. In Mississippi he supervised the black church's missions and served as a presiding elder. Stringer's great talent was organization. "Wherever he went in the state," Vernon Lane Wharton has written, "churches, lodges, benevolent societies, and political machines sprang up and flourished." He played a prominent role in the Mississippi Constitutional Convention in 1868. After 1869 Stringer's influence in state politics began to wane. His place as chief spokesman for the blacks was taken by James Lynch.[16]

Before coming to Mississippi, Lynch worked with the freedmen in South Carolina and Georgia. In 1866 he became the editor of the *Christian Recorder*, a post which he held for a little over a year. Resigning mysteriously in 1867, Lynch left the A.M.E. Church and went to Mississippi as

14. The following works examine the Republican and abolitionist campaign to enfranchise the freedmen: McPherson, *The Struggle for Equality*, Ch. 11; Lawanda Cox and John H. Cox, *Politics, Principle, and Prejudice, 1865–1866* (New York: Free Press, 1963), Chs. 8–10. The following issues of the *Christian Recorder* also criticize the government for failing to enfranchise the freedmen: July 8, 1865; August 12, 1865; September 9, 1865; November 11, 1865. For some other criticisms of Johnson's treatment of Negroes see *The Semi-Centenary and the Retrospection of the A.M.E. Church in the U.S.A.*, 159, 169.
15. Biographical references for these men will be found in the following notes in this chapter: 15, 17, 18, 19, 21, 23, 24, 25, 26, 27, 28.
16. Vernon Lane Wharton, *The Negro in Mississippi, 1865–1890* (1947; reprinted New York: Harper Torch Book, 1965), 149. See his Chapter 3 for Lynch's biography.

a minister of the Methodist Episcopal Church, North. In Mississippi Lynch served as the presiding elder of the Jackson District and also worked as an assistant in the Education Department of the Freedmen's Bureau. These two positions enabled him to wield considerable influence over Mississippi blacks. In 1869 the rapport which he had developed with the blacks and his connections in the Republican party helped him win a contest for secretary of state. "Let the people in Mississippi rally to his support, and to the support of the whole Republican ticket," the *Recorder* urged. "Let no personal feelings lead any of our people to scratch off the name of the prospective secretary. . . . Let us not vote our Church, but our party." Such endorsements no doubt contributed to Lynch's victory, since the political preferences of a number of the freedmen seem to have been influenced by their religious affiliations.

As secretary of state, Lynch played an active role in Mississippi politics. He was idolized by the freedmen and maintained good relations with his opponents in the Democratic party. Initially his relations with the Republicans were good, but by 1872 they appear to have deteriorated. When he received the party's nomination for Congress in 1875, some of his white Republican rivals, jealous of his success, had him taken to court on a charge of adultery. The ensuing scandal caused Lynch to lose the nomination and he died shortly after this, his friends said of a broken heart.[17]

Another A.M.E. cleric who held public office in Mississippi was Hiram Rhodes Revels. He was born in Fayetteville, North Carolina, September

17. Wharton, *The Negro in Mississippi, 1865–1890*, 54–55; Smith, *A History of the A.M.E. Church*, 46; *Christian Recorder*, October 30, 1869; see the *Christian Recorder* for February 11, 1865, for Lynch's criticisms of the church's hierarchy. See also the debate which he participated in concerning the church's name. Lynch wanted to drop the word *African* from the church's title. *Christian Recorder*, December 19, 1863; November 21, 1863; April 9, 1864; *New Orleans Tribune*, June 9, 1865. For the opposing point of view see *Christian Recorder*, April 16, 1864; April 8, 1865; October 30, 1869. A.M.E. ministers used their pulpits to politicize their congregations. See, for example, the comments about this in the New York *Times*, July 3, 1874; *The Condition of Affairs in the Late Insurrectionary States*, VII, 1034 and XIII, 171; Atlanta *Constitution*, November 28, 1868; and Sweet, "Methodist Church Influence in Southern Politics." William C. Harris, "James Lynch: Black Leader in Southern Reconstruction," *Historian*, XXXIV (1971), 40–61. This article suggests that before his death Lynch's influence among the freedmen was declining. Stories of his taste for strong liquor were beginning to undermine his reputation with the black community. For the interpretation that Lynch died of a broken heart, see Wharton, *The Negro in Mississippi, 1865–1890*, 155.

1, 1827. His parents, who were free persons of color, sent him to an elementary school run by a black woman. After completing his education in this school, Revels studied at seminaries in Indiana and Ohio. He then entered the ministry of the A.M.E. Church and held prominent charges in Indiana, Illinois, Ohio, Missouri, and Maryland. Revels' career in the A.M.E. Church was temporarily halted in 1854 when the congregation he was pastoring in St. Louis was torn apart by internal bickering. Conditions in the congregation reached a low point on October 18, 1854, when its members rioted. Disturbed by the behavior of the blacks, the mayor of the city closed the church and refused to reopen it until Bishop Payne came to St. Louis and adjudicated the dispute. Payne's decision caused Revels to leave the church. He soon joined the Presbyterian Church and was sent to Baltimore, where he worked until the outbreak of the Civil War. Once hostilities commenced, Revels helped organize the first Negro regiments in Maryland and Missouri. In 1864, feeling that his health was failing, he resigned his position in the Presbyterian Church and went South; reunited with the A.M.E. Church, Revels became presiding elder of the Natchez District. Upon arriving in Mississippi, he was asked to work with the Freedmen's Bureau. He accepted the offer and his efforts to aid the freedmen impressed General Adelbert Ames, the military governor of the state, who appointed him to the city council. Drawn into politics against his will, Revels ran for the state senate in 1869 and was elected. His tenure as a state senator was brief because his colleagues, impressed with his work, elected him to the United States Senate to serve out the unexpired term of Jefferson Davis. Revels' accomplishments as a United States senator were few. Although he did speak on several occasions, none of the legislation which he introduced was passed. After his term expired, he returned to Mississippi, left the A.M.E. Church, and became a minister in the M.E. Church, North.[18]

In Florida, seven A.M.E. ministers served in the state legislature and a

18. The date which Revels gives for his birth is contested by two of his biographers. He says that he was born in 1827 and they cite 1822 as the year of his birth. I have used the date given by Revels in Joseph A. Borome (ed.), "The Autobiography of Hiram Rhodes Revels Together with Some Letters By and About Him," *Midwest Journal*, V (1952–53), 79–92. These two works cite the 1822 date: J. F. Shaw, *The Negro in the History of Methodism* (Nashville: Parthenon Press, 1954), 146; Alexander W. Wayman, *Cyclopaedia of African Methodism*, 101–102. For Revels' difficulties with Bishop Payne, see *Recollections of Seventy Years*, 122–23.

few held offices on the local level. Biographical data for five of these men is limited. Little is known, for example, about Josiah Armstrong, who was born in Lancaster, Pennsylvania, May 30, 1842, and emigrated to Florida as a young man. In Florida he joined the A.M.E. Church, which in 1869 ordained him as a deacon and the following year made him an elder. Although he was elected to the legislature in 1871–1872, and again in 1875–1876, Armstrong played a minor role in legislative affairs. This also may be true of William S. Bradwell, the A.M.E. minister who converted Armstrong. A former slave, Bradwell was born in Darien, Georgia; he worked as a slave preacher before emancipation, became a minister of the A.M.E. Church in 1866, and was sent to Florida to work with the freedmen. Bradwell exerted significant influence over his charges, was elected to the Florida Constitutional Convention of 1868, and served in the state senate from 1868–1870. In the convention he aligned himself with the moderates, as he appears to have done during his senatorial career. William A. Stewart served in the Florida house in 1873–1874. Little more is known about him except that he "was respected locally for his modest lamb-like nature." Equally little is known about Stewart's contemporary H. S. Harmon, the first black man admitted to the Florida bar. Harmon was both a minister and a lawyer. Combining these professions, he championed the rights of his people.[19]

A great deal more is known about the other three A.M.E. ministers who held public office in Florida. Thomas Warren Long, for instance, was born near Jacksonville in 1832. When the Civil War began, he ran off and joined the Union army in Fernandina. Long later returned to the Jacksonville area and helped his wife and daughter escape from slavery. When the war was over, he returned to Florida and entered the ministry of the A.M.E. Church. He advanced rapidly in the church's hierarchy and by 1870 was presiding elder of the Jacksonville District. As a popular minis-

19. Joe Richardson in his book *The Negro in the Reconstruction of Florida, 1865–1877* (Tallahassee: Florida State University Press, 1965), states that five ministers were elected to the legislature but he lists six (see pages 94–95, 193). Jerrell H. Shofner in his book *Nor Is It Over Yet: Florida in the Era of Reconstruction, 1863–1877* (Gainesville: The University Presses of Florida, 1974), suggests that Bardwell favored separate schools for blacks, p. 173). Quoted in Richardson, *The Negro in the Reconstruction of Florida,* 69, 95, 189, 196. For a superb analysis of A.M.E. ministers in Florida politics during Reconstruction, see Robert L. Hall, "The Gospel According to Radicalism: African Methodism Comes to Tallahassee After the Civil War," *Apalachee,* VIII (1971–1979), 69–81. This essay supports a number of the observations made in this chapter.

ter of the A.M.E. Church, he received the political support of the blacks in his district. Long served in the Florida senate from 1873–1876.[20]

If Long's career was a success, Robert Meachum's was even more of one. Born of mixed parentage in Quincy, Florida, around 1836, Meachum was raised in a home where his father owned him and his mother, a slave woman. He learned to read and write, even though his father was forced to withdraw him from a white school when students objected to his presence. When his father died, Meachum became the property of his father's sister-in-law. After the slaves were freed, Meachum became a minister and organized the first A.M.E. congregation in Tallahassee in 1865. Two years later he began his career in politics as voter registrar of Jefferson County. The next year he was a delegate to the constitutional convention. As a minister-politician, Meachum was to hold numerous offices, some of them concurrently. Throughout Reconstruction he served in the state senate and held other offices at the same time. In 1868, for example, he was a Republican presidential elector and the clerk of the circuit court of Jefferson County. From 1868–1870 Meachum held the office of superintendent of schools in Jefferson County, and after a hiatus of three years he held the office again from 1873–1875. In 1874 he made an unsuccessful bid for a seat in the United States House of Representatives. As a state senator Meachum was an effective legislator. His efforts to help the freedmen provoked Klan opposition, and at least one attempt was made on his life.[21]

The most prominent A.M.E. minister-politician in Florida during Reconstruction was Charles H. Pearce. Although he never rose above the rank of elder in the church, Pearce was called "Bishop" because of the power he exercised over his followers. Born a slave in Queen Anne's County, Maryland, as a youth he purchased his freedom, and became a member of the A.M.E. Church. In 1852 he joined the New England Conference of the A.M.E. Church, but remained a member for only a short time. He resigned and went to Canada to work as a missionary, and he remained there until the war was over. At Bishop Payne's request, Pearce went to Florida and was extremely successful in getting the freedmen to join the A.M.E. Church. His work for the church made him a powerful figure in Leon County; in fact, he "dictated" who was to be on the county's delega-

20. Richardson, *The Negro in the Reconstruction of Florida*, 195.
21. *Ibid.*, 192.

tion to the constitutional convention of 1868. Pearce's political clout got him elected to the state senate, and he served there from 1868–1872.[22]

In South Carolina there were four A.M.E. ministers active in politics on the state level. William E. Johnston of Sumter attended the organizing convention of the Republican party in South Carolina in 1867. A year later he was a delegate to the constitutional convention, and shortly after, he was elected to the South Carolina House of Representatives where he served as a representative from 1868–1869. Richard Valentine worked for the church in Abbeville and was a member of the state's first Republican legislature. Little else is known about him. His colleague, William M. Thomas, who also served in the legislature, is even more of an enigma.[23]

R. H. Cain ("Daddy Cain," as he was called by his detractors) was the most successful A.M.E. minister-politician in South Carolina. He was born in Greensboro County, Virginia, April 12, 1825. When Cain was a young man, he and his parents moved to Ohio, where Cain worked on a steamboat. He joined the A.M.E. Church in 1841 and three years later was licensed to preach. After this he held different appointments in the church and rose rapidly in the hierarchy. In 1865 Bishop Payne transferred him to the South Carolina Conference and stationed him in Charleston, as presiding elder. As head of the A.M.E. community in Charleston, Cain organized and built Emanuel Church, which was to become "one of the strongest political organizations in the state." He also organized another church and named it after Morris Brown, a former Charlestonian, who had been forced to flee during the Denmark Vesey Conspiracy. These churches and the others established by the A.M.E. ministers in the city formed the basis of Cain's political power. He was a delegate to the convention of 1868 and served one term in the state senate. He also edited a paper called the *Missionary Record*, which was simultaneously an organ of the Republican party and the A.M.E. Church. Retiring from the senate, he worked as a lobbyist in Columbia during the 1870–1871 session of the legislature. In 1872 he was elected to Congress and served from

22. Dorothy Dodd, "Bishop Pearce and the Reconstruction of Leon County," *Apalachee: Publication of the Tallahassee Historical Society* (1946) 5–12; Wayman, *Cyclopaedia of African Methodism*, 125.

23. Nancy Vance Ashmore, *The Development of the African Methodist Episcopal Church in South Carolina, 1865–1965* (M.A. thesis, University of South Carolina, 1969), 30; Wayman, *Cyclopaedia of African Methodism*, 89; Joel Williamson, *After Slavery* (Chapel Hill: The University of North Carolina Press, 1965), 368. Ashmore, *The Development of the African Methodist Episcopal Church in South Carolina*, 161.

1873–1875. Cain was not a candidate for office in 1875 but did run in 1876 and was elected to the forty-fifth Congress. He retired from public life in 1878 and devoted the rest of his career to church work.[24]

Nine A.M.E. ministers were delegates to the Georgia Constitutional Convention. Three of the men were elders in the church, Henry Strickland, Robert Cromby, and Henry M. Turner. The other six were deacons, Isaac Anderson, Robert Alexander, Thomas Craton, William H. Noble, John Whitaker, and M. Jones. After the convention only Henry Turner served in the legislature. Turner was the most outspoken minister-politician in the A.M.E. Church, and as events unfolded in the South, he became extremely dissatisfied with the Republican party and with the United States. But all of this lay in the future. On New Year's Day, 1866, Turner was still optimistic as he addressed the congregation of the Springfield Baptist Church in Augusta, Georgia, telling the assemblage that this was the first day of a new era. "This day, which hereto separated so many families, and tear wet so many faces; heaved so many hearts, and filled the air with so many groans and sighs; this of all others the most bitter day of the year to our poor miserable race, shall henceforth and forever be filled with acclamations of the wildest joy, and expressions of ecstasy too numerous for angelic pens to note." Turner concluded his speech by reminding the congregation of the love which resided in the black man's heart. "The fact is, we have a better heart than white people. We want them free and invested with all their rights. We went to treat them kindly and live in friendship; . . . as soon as old things can be forgotten, or all things become common . . . the Southern people will take us by the hands and welcome us to their respect and regard."[25]

Turner was born on May 1, 1834, near Newberry Courthouse, South Carolina. His parents were free Negroes. After her husband's death Mrs. Turner's small income forced her to bond her son to a local planter. As a bonded servant, Turner learned the trades of blacksmith and carriage maker, and he was required to work with the slaves in the fields. When the overseer tried to whip him, Turner, knowing that he was free born

24. *A.M.E. Church Review*, III (1886), 338–50; *Biographical Directory of the American Congress, 1774–1971* (Washington: Government Printing Office, 1971), 689; Wayman, *Cyclopaedia of African Methodism*, 11; Wright, *The Bishops of the A.M.E. Church*, 119.
25. *Christian Recorder*, December 28, 1867. Biographical data for these men, other than Turner, is lacking; Savannah *Colored American*, January 13, 1866.

and could never legally be reduced to slavery, was said to have fought back.

Turner's elementary education consisted of private instruction by friends in South Carolina. As it was unlawful to teach Negroes to read and write, community pressure finally forced these friends to cease their instruction. Left alone, he learned to read by himself. When he was fifteen, Turner secured employment as an office boy in a law firm in Abbeville, South Carolina. His employers were impressed with his ability to learn and allowed him to borrow their books; they also tutored him in mathematics, history, Bible studies, geography, and astronomy.

In 1848 Turner joined the Methodist Episcopal Church, South; in 1853 he was licensed to preach, and he achieved the highest rank held by a Negro in that church prior to the Civil War. During the next five years Turner worked as a missionary among slaves and free Negroes in South Carolina, Georgia, Alabama, Louisiana, and Missouri. On a visit to New Orleans in 1857, Turner met Dr. Willis R. Revels, a Negro physician and a minister in the A.M.E. Church. Revels spoke to Turner about the work of his church and the desire of the church's ministry "to develop their church life on an independent basis, free from any supervision by white ministers who might be disposed to curb the development of race consciousness or hinder the Negro in his efforts at development and self-expression." Sometime during the next year Turner resigned his position in the Methodist Episcopal Church, South and was admitted to the Missouri Annual Conference of the A.M.E. Church. Shortly afterward, Turner went to Baltimore, where he served as a minister for four years. The slave codes of most southern states prohibited the A.M.E. Church from ministering to the mass of Negroes. Turner, therefore, decided to prepare himself for missionary service in Africa. Friends who taught at Trinity College in Baltimore instructed him·in most of the regular college subjects, and ministers tutored him in Hebrew, Latin, and Greek.[26]

The outbreak of the Civil War altered Turner's plans. Instead of going to Africa, he decided to pursue his ministry in the South. During Reconstruction, Turner would renew his interest in Africa because of the deteriorating position of Negroes in American society. In 1862 Turner presided over the largest Negro church in Washington, the Israel Metropolitan

26. Quoted in Minton J. Batten, "Henry M. Turner, Negro Bishop Extraordinary," *Church History*, VII (1938), 235.

Church. In his capacity as a minister, he invited Benjamin Wade and Thaddeus Stevens to address the congregation on current racial and political issues, and he advocated the enlistment of Negroes in the Union army. When his advice resulted in the creation of a Negro regiment, Turner agreed to become its chaplain. After the war, President Johnson appointed Turner a chaplain in the regular army and assigned him to the Freedmen's Bureau in Georgia. Turner resigned after only a few months of service because bureau officers objected to his organizing A.M.E. congregations while working for the government. His activities as a Republican organizer received official approval in 1867, when he was appointed by the National Republican Executive Committee to superintend the organization of colored people in Georgia.

After serving as a delegate to the Georgia Constitutional Convention, Turner was elected to the legislature. Along with the other Negro members, he was expelled six weeks after the legislative session opened. In 1869, Turner was appointed postmaster of Macon but was forced to resign when several white citizens of Macon charged him with moral turpitude. The last public office held by Turner was in the Georgia legislature of 1870.[27]

While Turner was working in the state government, another A.M.E. minister served on the Atlanta City Council. William Finch, born a slave in Washington, Wilkes County, Georgia, around 1832, was apprenticed as a youth to a tailor and learned his trade. During the war he remained on his master's plantation, but when the war was over, he moved his family to Augusta and opened a tailor shop. Finch lived in Augusta for two years, but business was poor there, and he barely made enough money to support his family. Moving to Atlanta in 1868, Finch prospered and became an important figure in Atlanta's black community. He was elected to the city council in 1870 and served one term. As a councilman Finch urged the city to establish public schools for blacks and to hire black teachers. He also fought for causes which would benefit all of the city's citizens regardless of race.[28]

In addition to serving in state and local governments in the South,

27. E. Merton Coulter, "Henry M. Turner," *Negro Legislators in Georgia* (Athens: Georgia Historical Quarterly, 1968), 52.
28. Clarence A. Bacote, "William Finch, Negro Councilman, and Political Activities in Atlanta During Early Reconstruction," *Journal of Negro History*, XL (1955), 341–352.

A.M.E. ministers also held posts in the Freedmen's Bank. Theophilus G. Stewart was the president of the Freedmen's Savings Bank of Macon, Georgia, in 1869. Stewart was a northerner who had been born and educated in New Jersey. In 1864 he joined the Philadelphia Conference of the A.M.E. Church. A year later he was transferred to the South Carolina Conference where he worked for several years before being sent to Georgia. While working as a missionary in South Carolina and Georgia, Stewart also served as an army chaplain. In Georgia he built the A.M.E. Church in Macon and served as presiding elder of that district. The other A.M.E. minister employed by the bank was George Brodie, the church's superintendent of missionary work in North Carolina.[29]

Embarking on a career in politics was not easy for these men. They faced opposition from southern whites and from some of their cohorts. The presiding bishop of the A.M.E. Church, Daniel Alexander Payne, "took no special interest in politics," one of the church's historians has written, "outside of what pertained to the duties of citizenship." In his history of the church, Payne expressed a muted dissatisfaction with those ministers who became politicos: "The only apology which can be made for them," he wrote, "is that for intelligence and organizing power their equals could not be found in the laity, hence politics laid hold of them and by a kind of conscription forced them into the army of politicians." At the General Conference of 1872, a faction within the church hierarchy expressed similar discontent by introducing the following resolution: "That it is the opinion of this conference that it is detrimental to the interest of our church for our ministers to engage in politics, and that no one shall be allowed to be so engaged whilst holding a charge in [the] church." The resolution was tabled and never became church law. If it had, some of the more prominent minister-politicians would have left the church, or flouted the ruling; for they believed that politicizing the freedmen was a minister's duty since it was necessary for the ex-slave's survival.[30]

To politicize the freedmen, A.M.E. ministers used their church's hier-

29. Smith, *A History of the African Methodist Episcopal Church*, 85; Wayman, *Cyclopaedia of African Methodism*, 155; Payne, *History of the African Methodist Episcopal Church*, 470–71.
30. Quoted in Charles Spencer Smith, *The Life of Daniel Alexander Payne* (Nashville: A.M.E. Publishing House, 1894), 45; Payne, *History of the African Methodist Church*, 470–71; *Journal of the Fifteenth Quadrennial Session of the General Conference of the African Methodist Episcopal Church, Held in Nashville, Tennessee, May 6, 1872* (n.p.), 134.

archical structure. Methodism, with its units of class, society, and band, provided the ministers with an organizational structure they could use for political purposes. This was particularly true of the class, which in some ways corresponded to the organization of a modern political party.[31] These meetings and the regular church services provided the minister-politicians with an arena for dissemination of their political and religious ideas. Using gestures, physical expressions, and language rich in simile and metaphor, the ministers were able to stir congregations and political rallies. Most importantly, these ministers provided the freedmen, who were looking for leadership, with an alternative to their former masters.[32]

To break the slave owners' psychological hold on their former chattel, ministers of the A.M.E. Church attacked the idea that God was white. Henry M. Turner preached a sermon entitled "God Is Not White"; and as presiding elder and later bishop in Georgia, he forbade the congregations in his district to sing the hymn, "Lord Wash Me and I Shall Be Whiter Than Snow." In South Carolina, the Reverend William E. Johnston was accused of telling a meeting at Fleming's Sheltor Church, Sumter County, "Christ is an African, born in Africa and preached his first sermon in Africa. Mary his mother was a black woman, and Joseph his father an African and black man." The minister-politicians were quite successful in their efforts to proselytize the freedmen; for example, by the late 1860s in South Carolina the church had 30,000 members. In Florida the number of members increased from 4,798 in 1868 to 13,102 in 1874–1875. The Alabama Annual Conference also grew quickly during this time. In 1868, when the conference was organized, it contained six churches and 5,616

31. William Nisbet Chambers and Walter Dean Burnham (eds.), *The American Party Systems: Stages of Political Development* (2nd ed.; New York: Oxford University Press, 1975), 5. See also Chapter 2 of Maurice Duverger, *Political Parties* (New York: Science Editions, John Wiley & Sons, Inc., 1963), particularly pages 71–79, for criterion of membership.
32. Barclay, *To Reform the Nation*, 337–39. On this point see the suggestive comments of Mike Thelwell in his essay "Back with the Wind: Mr. Styron and the Reverend Turner," in John Henrik Clarke (ed.), *Ten Black Writers Respond* (Boston: Beacon Press, 1968), 80–81; Bruce Rosenberg, *The Art of the American Folk Preachers* (New York: Oxford University Press, 1970). For an example of a minister urging his colleagues to use their pulpits to diffuse "sound principles of political economy to their congregations," see the New Orleans *Tribune*, July 21, 1864. For role of Methodists in the politicization of the South during Reconstruction, see three articles by William W. Sweet: "The Methodist Episcopal Church and Reconstruction," "Methodist Church Influence in Southern Politics," and "Negro Churches in the South: A Phase of Reconstruction," *Methodist Review*, CIV (1921), 405–18.

members; by 1872 there were sixty-six churches and 10,558 members.[33]

Wherever they lived, A.M.E. members voted for the Republican candidate at their minister's behest. Ministers of the church did not apologize for their political activities. Usually the most educated men in their communities, the ministers believed that they were fulfilling their responsibilities to their people. The manner in which they combined politics and religion, however, angered southern whites. Carlton B. Cole, a Georgia Superior Court judge, testified before a congressional committee that Negro preachers not only controlled their congregations but frequently preached political sermons. His testimony was corroborated by another witness who was a bit more tolerant. Although he conceded that black preachers gave political advice, he pointed out that their white ministers did also. Before the Civil War and after, white ministers had offered political opinions from the pulpit. Black ministers were only conforming to an established practice. The significant difference, however, was that A.M.E. ministers attempted to broaden their appeal to politicize both *blacks* and *whites* in the South.[34]

3   Although evidence is often fragmentary, some generalizations can be made about A.M.E. ministers who were active in state politics. Typical is the political career of Henry M. Turner, the most outspoken of the A.M.E. minister-politicians. By looking at the successes and failures of his foray into politics, it is possible to arrive at some understanding of what it meant to be a black politician during Reconstruction.[35]

In general A.M.E. ministers supported legislation which would give education, relief, and suffrage to both races. They acted in a spirit of good will which they hoped would not alienate the whites. In South Carolina,

33. Quoted in Wright, *Bishops of the A.M.E. Church*, 33. *Sumter Watchman*, September 29, 1860, cited in a footnote in Francis B. Simkins and Robert H. Woody, *South Carolina During Reconstruction* (Chapel Hill: The University of North Carolina Press, 1932), 411; Williamson, *After Slavery* (Chapel Hill: University of North Carolina Press, 1965), 369; Peter Kolchin, *First Freedom* (Westport: Greenwood Press, 1972), 111; See *Christian Recorder*, April 20, 1967; November 2, 1867, for statements about black support for Republicans.
34. *The Condition of Affairs in the Late Insurrectionary States*, VII, 1184 and 1132; see also the comments about Negro preachers and politics in Richardson, *The Negro in the Reconstruction of Florida*.
35. My choice of Turner is dictated by the fact that I found more information about his career than any of the other men discussed in this section.

for example, R. H. Cain opposed a school bill which included provisions for integration and for compulsory attendance. His opposition may have reflected a fear that these provisions would exacerbate racial tensions. William Bradwell, one of Florida's black representatives, also opposed mixed schools in his state, apparently for a similar reason.[36]

Underlying these efforts at racial harmony was the belief that the future of the South depended upon interracial cooperation. Black ministers tried to calm white fears that Negro freedom would lead to racial amalgamation. In Georgia, Henry M. Turner told a crowd of blacks, "Instead of them fearing we will marry their daughters and sisters, we should fear and tremble for our daughters and sisters, for we have a thousand specimens of the latter to one of the former." And addressing a black crowd on the Fourth of July, in Macon, Georgia, James Lynch posed a question to the white South:

> Why hate the colored race? They have tilled your lands and made them bring forth the great staples that have enriched you, affording luxurious comforts; they have nursed your children in infancy and toiled for them while at school and college; they have ever rejoiced when you rejoiced, sorrowed when you sorrowed; meekly and submissively they have borne your restrictions, punishments, and cruelties; they have followed the armies of Beauregard, Wade Hampton and Lee and others, and borne your sons from the gory field, to a place of safety and staunched their bleeding wounds.

A similar selflessness, Lynch said, would characterize the former slaves now that they were free, because they harbored "no feelings of malice for their former masters." In promising that the freedmen would not be vindictive, Lynch articulated one of the cardinal tenets of his people's faith. A spiteful attitude would reduce them to the level of their oppressors and tarnish the righteousness of their cause. Having perceived the war as a

---

36. Richardson, *The Negro in the Reconstruction of Florida*, 189; *Proceedings of The Constitutional Convention of South Carolina* (1868; reprinted New York: Arno Press and New York *Times*, 1968), 196, 381, 382, 418, 421, 693, 830, 831; Ethel Maude Christler, *Participation of Negroes in the Government of Georgia, 1867–1870* (M.A. thesis, Atlanta University, 1932), 23, 64, 69; *Proceedings of the Constitutional Convention of South Carolina*, 693. These kinds of fears did not inhibit Charles Pearce in Florida. As a member of a committee on education, he blocked a public school bill until one was drafted which did not prohibit integration. Richardson, *The Negro in the Reconstruction of Florida*, 173. Shofner, *Nor Is It Over Yet: Florida in the Era of Reconstruction*, 173.

struggle between the forces of light and those of darkness, the minister-politicians and their constituents were disposed to treat southern whites in an equitable manner. Their side had triumphed, and it was incumbent upon them to be charitable. This spirit of altruism would prove both a great strength and a great weakness. Although the A.M.E. ministers' politics were rooted in Christian principles, they were neither religious fanatics nor cynics. Rather, they acted as all men do, within a frame of ideas which gave meaning and direction to their lives.[37]

The key to understanding Henry M. Turner's activities during Reconstruction and after lies in his theological interpretation of Negro history. "God seeing the African stand in need of civilization, sanctioned for a while the slave trade, not that it was in harmony with his fundamental laws for one man to rule another, nor did he ever contemplate that the Negro was to be reduced to the status of a vassal, but as a subject for moral and intellectual culture." The Africans, Turner argued, had been committed to the care of white men "as a trust from God." According to the rules of the trust, the Africans were to work and help to build the nation, while their white masters clothed, fed, and educated them. Nonetheless, the whites chose to violate the rules of the trust and reduced the Negro to the level of a beast in the field. Slavery proved to be a "reactionary curse" for white southerners. "It rebounded back upon the white man while it degraded the status of the black. . . . Trafficking in human blood, buying and selling, separating man and wife, parents and children, hardened the hearts and numbed the consciousness of whites and made them cruel and wicked." If the South had only been obeyed the rules of God's trust, the Civil War could have been avoided and "slavery would have passed away so imperceptibly that no one would have felt the shock."[38]

The logic of his theory of Negro history led Turner to see Reconstruction as a conversion experience: White people would undergo a change of heart and reorient their attitudes and beliefs. Turner believed that white people had nothing to fear from Negroes: "Unlike the white man, we have no desire to enslave or deprive them of their oaths, disenfranchise them, or

37. *Christian Recorder*, December 14, 1861; James Lynch, *The Mission of the United States Republic: An Oration July 4, 1865* (Augusta, Ga.: *Chronicle & Sentinel* Office, 1865), 11. Also see on this point R. H. Cain's comments on why he came South and his feelings towards whites in *Proceedings of the Constitutional Convention of South Carolina*, 137, 138, 421.
38. Savannah *Colored American*, January 13, 1866.

expatriate them." What the Negro wanted was equal opportunity and equal treatment.[39]

To achieve this goal of equality, Turner, as a delegate to the Georgia Constitutional Convention of 1867–1868, introduced and voted for resolutions which aided the planter class. He introduced two resolutions which sought to stabilize the economic life of the state by affording relief to the planters: One would have prevented the sale of property of owners who were unable to pay their taxes; the other resolution provided relief for banks. Turner also voted for resolutions petitioning Congress to grant or appropriate thirty million dollars for planter relief and for legislation requiring the ability to read English intelligently as a qualification for suffrage. Perhaps his most surprising act, however, was his move to have the convention take up a petition for the pardon of Jefferson Davis. The motion failed.[40]

When he was elected to the legislature, Turner introduced a number of bills which dealt with state issues. The first bill established a state police force, the second gave women the vote, and the third created a public school system. With the exception of women's suffrage, none of these measures can be characterized as revolutionary or radical. He did not, for example, advocate the confiscation and redistribution of land. His quiescence on this point contrasted sharply with the position taken by other black leaders. In Louisiana, for instance, the publishers of the *Tribune* advocated the destruction of the plantation system. Such a move, they believed, would bring about a domestic revolution in the South and curb the power of the antebellum slave-owning aristrocracy. "The planters are no longer needed in the character of masters . . . [and] our basis for labor must now be put on a democratic footing. There is no more room, in the organization of our society, for an oligarchy of slaveholders, [or even] of property holders." These sentiments, although expressed by middleclass Negro newspaper publishers, reflected the desire of the freedmen to own their own land. General Saxton, the head of the Freedmen's Bureau in Georgia, noted that: "The object which the freedmen have most at heart is the purchase of land. They all desire to get small homesteads and

39. *Ibid.*
40. See John Hope Franklin, *Reconstruction: After the Civil War* (Chicago: University of Chicago Press, 1961), 91. See also Allen D. Candler, *The Confederate Records of the State of Georgia*, IV (Atlanta: n.p., 1911), 243, 290, 470–71, 480, 559.

locate themselves upon them, and there is scarcely any sacrifice too great for them to accomplish this object." Despite the widespread desire among the freedmen for property, Turner did not concern himself with the issue of land reform. Not only did he fail to advocate confiscation, Turner also neglected more moderate possibilities. For example, he could have resisted efforts to grant the planters relief. This tactic would have made land available for the freedmen to purchase. Turner's failure to pursue land reform therefore raises questions about his dealings with the Republican party, with white southerners, and with his black constituents.[41]

During Reconstruction, Turner was confident that the Negro would improve his political, social, and economic position in southern society. "Human disenthrallment," Turner observed, "seems to have been in all ages of the world, the special agency of God's administration. All great convulsive courses have been succeeded with liberative consequences." The belief that conditions would improve influenced his initial relations with white Republicans and white southerners and explains his failure to advocate land redistribution. He did not want to antagonize his Republican allies or the old planter class. Private property, Turner realized, was sacrosanct. In advocating the confiscation and redistribution of land he would have been ahead of his Republican allies. Most important of all, Turner never occupied a position which would have given him sufficient power to initiate a policy of land redistribution.

From the beginning of Reconstruction, Turner tried to win the support of white Georgians. He sought to allay their fears about miscegenation. He assured the whites that "no man in Georgia has been more conservative than I. Anything to please the white folks has been my motto, and so closely have I adhered to that course, that many among my own party have classed me as a Democrat." What the Negro wanted from the white southerner was simply "equal rights and equal justice before the law."

41. W. E. B. Du Bois, *Black Reconstruction* (New York: Russell & Russell, 1935), 505–506. For an example of a preacher-politician who favored land redistribution, see E. M. Coulter's article, "Aaron Alporia Bradley," in *Negro Legislators in Georgia* (Athens: *Georgia Historical Quarterly*, 1968), 37–120; August Meier, "Negroes in the First and Second Reconstruction," *Civil War History*, XIII (1967), 119. Quoted in Roger W. Shugg, *Origins of the Class Struggle in Louisiana* (Baton Rouge: Louisiana State University, 1939), 215–16; also in Manuel Gottlieb, "The Land Question in Georgia During Reconstruction," *Science and Society*, III (1959), 357–58. See for example R. H. Cain's speech on this subject in *Proceedings of the Constitutional Convention of South Carolina*, 10.

That these goals were never attained was the result not only of growing white opposition but also of a lack of unity in the Negro community.[42]

Within the black community of the postbellum South, Turner was a member of an educated elite. Servility and bondage created a number of social problems within the Negro community. "Slavery," Turner preached, "tended to make us thievish because we regarded it right to filch what we should have had as the reward of our labor. It also tended to make us untruthful, telling lies to escape punishment." To counteract these problems Turner advocated a program of self-help and improvement among his constituents. As a preacher in the African Methodist Episcopal Church, Turner established a number of schools because he believed that education was the primary need of the freedmen. Turner also had to deal with the problem of color prejudice within the Negro community. (In New Orleans, for example, the mulatto barbers would not cut the hair of the dark complexioned Negro members of the legislature.) Recognizing the divisiveness that color distinctions caused within the Negro community, Turner once cautioned his people: "[W]e want representative men, without regard to color, as long as they carry the brand of Negro oppression. . . . We need power and intellectual equality with whites. It does not matter whether he be a pretty or ugly Negro; a black Negro or a mulatto. Whether he were a slave or a free Negro; the question is, is he a Negro at all? If he be, let him go to work, be his personal appearance as deformed as a jackass, or as charming as Venus." Turner also told his listeners that "this Methodist, Baptist and Presbyterianism, and all other ists and isms must die out of our midst before we can come into power. We want power; it only comes through organization and organization comes through unity."[43]

Color, social, and religious divisions were not the only problems that Turner faced. The politicization of the Negro communities in Georgia and Louisiana produced factionalism, and the various Negro Republican factions often settled their differences in street brawls. During such difficulties, Turner served as a mediator. He knew that Negroes could not sur-

42. *Christian Recorder*, June 14, 1862. Quoted in Coulter, "Henry M. Turner," *Negro Legislators in Georgia*, 9; *Christian Recorder*, December 6, 1862; see also February 9, 1867.
43. *Colored American*, January 13, 1866; *Semi-Weekly Louisiana*, May 25, 1871; *Christian Recorder*, January 20, 1866.

vive politically in Georgia if they opposed each other. Turner's efforts to unify the blacks are indicative of his style of leadership.[44]

Turner's political leadership was more symbolic than substantive, however, because his power base was never strong enough to enable him to control or direct the Republican party. In Georgia, the A.M.E. Church served as the base for Turner's power. He described himself as "minister of the gospel and kind of politician." Combining these occupations, Turner was able to influence Georgia Negroes. He told a congressional committee: "Certainly, if any man in this country mingles with colored people I do. I am regarded as a prominent leader among them; I am presiding elder of a district, I have some twenty-seven preachers in my district. I hold from eight to ten camp meetings a year, where from two to three thousand people gather. There is not a week but what I am from forty to fifty, and a hundred to two hundred miles from home." The purpose of Turner's extensive travels in Georgia was to get Negroes to vote for the Republican party. He testified before a congressional committee that he "travelled a great deal" and took "a leading part in Republican politics, so far as colored men [were] concerned." On the subject of Negro office holding, Turner believed that only educated Negroes should hold office. He expected the Democratic party to nominate uneducated Negroes in order to discredit the idea of Negroes' holding office. "I have seen this ignoble piece of humanity, and tried to converse with him," Turner said of one such candidate, "but I found him to be so exceedingly low in the scale of intelligence that no one but a maniac could have been entertained by his wild farrago." Whether Turner was able to find educated Negroes to run for office is difficult to discern. The evidence suggests that he told Negroes to vote for white candidates when they had to choose between an educated white and an ignorant Negro. This policy, however, does not seem to have won him the respect or confidence of his white colleagues in the party.[45]

Born of expediency, Turner's alliance with the Republican party was bound to disintegrate. His break with the party began in 1868 when the

44. Coulter, "Henry M. Turner," *Negro Legislators in Georgia*, 7.
45. For the extent of Turner's missionary activities, see his description of his work in Edwin A. Redkey (ed.), *Respect Black: The Writing and Speeches of Henry McNeal Turner* (1863–1906; reprinted New York: Arno Press and New York *Times*, 1971), 30; *The Condition of Affairs in the Late Insurrectionary States*, VII, 1034, 1041, 1034; Coulter, "Henry M. Turner," in *Negro Legislators in Georgia*, 8.

Georgia legislature expelled its Negro members, including Turner, on the grounds that Negroes, though guaranteed the right to vote, had not been specifically made eligible for office, Before he left the legislature, Turner made what was probably the greatest speech of his career. He would not "fawn or cringe before them," Turner told his white listeners. "I was not aware that there was in the character of the [Anglo-Saxon] race so much cowardice . . . pusillanimity . . . [and] treachery." It was the Negroes who had started "the ball of liberty rolling in the state of Georgia . . . and [yet] there are persons in this legislature, today, who are ready to spit their poison in my face, while they themselves . . . opposed the ratification of the Constitution. They question my right to a seat in this body." Turner then set forth the Negro's claim:

> The great question is this. Am I a man? If I am such, I claim the rights of a man. Am I not a man because I happen to be of darker hue than honorable gentlemen around me? . . . Why, sir, though we are not white, we have accomplished much. We have pioneered civilization here; we have built up your country; we have worked in your fields, and garnered your harvest for two hundred and fifty years. And what do we ask of you in return . . . ? Do we ask retaliation? We ask it not . . . but we ask you now for our RIGHTS. It is extraordinary that a race such as yours, professing gallantry, and chivalry, and education and superiority, living in a land where ringing chimes call child and sire to the Church of God—a land . . . where courts of justice are presumed to exist . . . can make war upon the poor defenseless black man.

> You may expel us, gentlemen, but I firmly believe that you will some-day repent it. The black man cannot protect a country, if the country doesn't protect him; and if, tomorrow a war should arise, I would not raise a musket to defend a country where my manhood is de-nied. . . . You may expel us . . . but while you do it remember that there is a just God in Heaven, whose All-Seeing Eye beholds alike the acts of the oppressor and the oppressed, and who, despite the machinations of the wicked, never fails to vindicate the cause of justice.[46]

46. Henry M. Turner, *Speech on the Eligibility of Colored Men to Seats in the Georgia Legislature . . . September 3, 1868* (Augusta: n.p., 1868).

It may well have been Turner's expulsion from the legislature that disillusioned and radicalized him. Between 1868–1874 Turner underwent a significant change of attitude and outlook. On October 7, 1868, he was a delegate to a Negro convention in Macon, called to protest the expulsion of Negroes from the Georgia legislature. The next year (1869) he attended a convention called to organize "Negroes into a labor union to control prices." These attempts at economic and political organization suggest that Turner had not yet completely lost faith in America. But when the government failed to protect the Negro, that faith rapidly dissipated.

> This seems to be the only government on the earth that cannot protect its citizens, every few weeks the cry of insurrection comes from Louisiana, Georgia, Mississippi, etc., and a hecatomb of innocent people must be sacrificed to justify the accursed lie. And yet when you appeal to the government for protection, it is so weak and powerless it cannot give any. It is assumed to have the right and power to free the Negro, but it is weak as water when he calls upon it, to save him from hellish assassin. A country that can't protect its own supporters and defenders ought to go to pieces; it does not deserve the name of nation, nor ought it to stand twenty-four hours. I almost hate the land that gave me birth; and if there is not a speedy change, I shall publicly proclaim myself a rebel to my so-called country.

Turner could no longer tell Negroes, "let us love the whites and let bygones be by-gones, neither taunt nor insult them for past grievances, respect them; honor them; work for them; but still let us be men." Turner now advocated African emigration and told Negroes they could not be men in the United States.[47]

The failure of the government to pass the Civil Rights bill of 1874 apparently made Turner an advocate of African emigration. In a letter to the *Christian Recorder*, he noted a number of reasons why the bill had not passed and warned that further delay would endanger the Republican party in the South. Several months later, Turner wrote that "unless even-handed justice is dealt out to the Negro race, so far as the nation's laws can give it, the country will be racked by another war." He warned that

47. Atlanta *Constitution*, October 10, 1868; October 23, 1869; *Christian Recorder*, November 25, 1875; Savanah *Colored American*, January 13, 1866.

"things are tending to a crisis with our people . . . which many able colored men do not yet believe." Finally, he issued a manifesto on December 17, 1874, which discussed African emigration as the only viable alternative to extermination. "Let us repair there, from the whole country and build up a power in wealth, education, religion, and moral and social refinement; then we will have credit for what we do."[48] Turner's advocacy of emigration was an indirect admission on his part that his policy of reconciliation had failed. The policy failed because Turner and the other Negro Republican leaders in Georgia never occupied positions of power in the party. Moreover, the party itself was flawed. The Republican party of Georgia was built primarily around the votes of Negroes and yeoman whites. Although the groups had similar economic interests and demands, these were not enough to hold the party together. Its members could not overcome a congeries of attitudes and values inherited from slavery.[49]

The failure of the Republican party embittered Turner, and he became critical of the party and its policy during Reconstruction. "The Republican Party freed us as a war measure, I grant, and not from choice," he told the Negroes. "And for some years after we were liberated, what was our status? We had no rights under heaven that was worth the snap of a finger; our condition was simply anomalous. . . . The government had it in its power to have given us homes . . . but when the government did resolve to confer upon us the great boon so indispensable to our manhood and existence, what was the *modus operandi* employed? . . . Instead of passing a law covering the whole affair at once, which was not only demanded by the contingencies of events, but which was right *per se*, we were thrown into a whirlpool of legal mazes, by the passage of the Reconstruction Acts." Turner's earlier reluctance to demand land for the freedmen had reflected his optimism that cooperation with white southerners and Republicans would lead to a better world for the Negro. Before he died Turner would see another of his illusions shattered.[50]

The Negro community responded with skepticism, if not outrage, to

48. *Christian Recorder*, April 30, 1874; November 19, 1874. See also comments in the paper about President Grant and the civil rights bill, November 19, 1874; *Christian Recorder*, December 17, 1874.
49. Elizabeth Studley Nathans, *Losing the Peace* (Baton Rouge: Louisiana State University Press, 1968). For an account by a participant see T. G. Steward, *Fifty Years in the Gospel Ministry*, 128.
50. *Christian Recorder*, November 11, 1875.

Turner's emigration scheme. Most Negro leaders called it impractical and urged the Negro masses to stand firm on southern soil and defend their rights. Such remonstrances, Turner argued, were not only foolish but they revealed an ignorance of conditions in the South. "The only reason why Africa is unpopular and ignored by some colored men is because of its unpopularity among whites . . . some of our leading men may blush and slur at Africa till their doomsday arrives. But God intends for us to carry and spread enlightenment and civilization over that land." What Turner envisioned was not a mass Negro exodus to Africa but rather the creation of a black Christian nation which would exemplify the race's achievements and be an inspiration to the unredeemed Negro.[51]

Turner made several trips to Africa but was never able to convince large numbers of Negroes that emigration would solve their problem. His last years were spent denouncing the United States. In 1906 he attracted nationwide attention when he proclaimed from a Macon platform that "to the Negro in this country, the American flag is a dirty and contemptible rag," and that "hell is an improvement over the United States when the Negro is involved." Turner died in 1915.[52]

Although it is not a paradigm, Turner's career suggests some of the hopes and aspirations which the minister-politicians entertained during Reconstruction. To fulfill their dreams of a reconstructed South, some of these men faced mobs, were threatened with assassination, and saw their churches burned. Throughout these difficulties the majority of them continued to believe that good would triumph over evil. Turner was an exception to this rule. He became disillusioned with the church's alliance with the Republican party quite early and tried to remind the Republicans of their responsibilities to the Negro and dependence on his votes in the South.[53]

By the 1870s the disillusionment which Turner expressed in the late 1860s was echoed by others in the church. These complaints reflected a

51. *Christian Recorder*, December 17, 1874; January 14, 1875; January 11, 1877; William J. Simmons, *Men of Mark* (1887; reprinted New York: Arno Press and New York *Times*, 1968), 817; Edwin Redkey, "Bishop Turner's African Dream," *Journal of American History*, LIV (1967), 277.
52. Quoted in Redkey, "Bishop Turner's African Dream," 290.
53. *Christian Recorder*, March 24, 1866; August 10, 1867; May 13, 1867; *The Condition of Affairs in the Late Insurrectionary States*, 1035; *Christian Recorder*, March 13, 1873; *Colored Tribune*, April 15, 1876; *Christian Recorder*, August 10, 1876; December 14, 1876.

growing awareness on the part of black churchmen that the party was using their people and that they were getting nothing in return. Angered by the shabby treatment which some black Republicans received, after they voted for Horace Greeley and Charles Sumner in the election of 1872, one A.M.E. cleric told the party that it could no longer count on the freedmen's vote. "Our vote for Grant, en masse, was the last payment on the old score of: Didn't we free you?" The debt, he said, was discharged and in the future blacks would vote "as free and sovereign American citizens ought to vote, for the candidate that promises best by the country." Another minister, after noting the destitute state in which the majority of freedmen lived, urged the party to purchase some of the land for sale in the states of South Carolina, Florida, Louisiana, and Mississippi. "If it were bought by the Republicans they could rent it to the colored voters," he declared. Such a policy, the preacher argued, would make the freedmen independent of their Democratic landlords who threatened to fire the blacks if they voted for the Republicans. Not wanting to support the Democrats, the freedmen would "not vote at all." Upset by the venality of some Republican politicians, other church spokesmen asked the party to disown these men, because they were only interested in self-aggrandizement. If the party was going to survive, one A.M.E. minister observed, it would have to have "leaders who [could not] be bribed or bought, with gold or stocks." Finally, disgusted with the party's evasion and unfulfilled promises, H. M. Turner announced its demise:

> It is with unusual pain, we are compelled to chronicle the sad news, that the great Republican Party, hero of many battles and author of National Sovereignty, American Freedom, Civil and Political rights and many other world renowned and heaven approved works, was slaughtered in the house of his friends, April 24, 1877. He had been indisposed for some years, being seriously afflicted by Negro haters, office seekers, dough faces, weathercocks, time servers, and large numbers of political hypocrites, false pretenders, and unprincipled vagabonds. Such a number of wounds and diseases all preying upon his system at once was too much to be resisted, and the political giant of the 19th century had to succumb to the inevitable.[54]

54. *Christian Recorder*, February 27, 1873; February 1, 1877; October 30, 1873; February 4, 1877; April 26, 1877.

In evaluating the church's social and political efforts in the South it would be easy to dismiss the entire exercise as a failure. To do so would be a great injustice. Although the ministers did not achieve their ultimate goal of an egalitarian society in the South, they did lay the foundation for a new community for the freedmen which served as a training ground for future leaders. Their political endeavors cannot, in fairness, be labeled as failures either. To say that they failed politically assumes that success was possible, that they might have succeeded had they been more politically astute. Given nineteenth-century American ideas about equality and race, complete success was highly unlikely. Indeed, in advocating that the Negro be granted civil and political equality, the black churchmen and their allies were ahead of their times.[55]

55. W. R. Brock, *An American Crisis* (New York: St. Martins Press 1963), 285; Fredrickson, *The Black Image in the White Mind*, 168, 182. For the church's conception of civil and political equality, see the resolution adopted at *The Fifteenth Quadrennial Session of the General Conference of the A.M.E. Church, May 6, 1872, Nashville, Tennessee* (n.p.), 74–75; see also the resolution adopted by the Florida Conference of the church in June, 1870. This resolution was entered as testimony in *The Condition of Affairs in the Late Insurrectionary States*, XIII, 170–71.

Epilogue

I began this essay by noting that the A.M.E. Church's mission to the slaves was a specific version of American "civil religion." As *A Rock in a Weary Land* has shown, this mission was neither a complete success nor a failure. When viewed in a broader context, it was a part of a process that Frederick Cooper has called "elevating the race." Throughout the nineteenth century those blacks who assumed a vanguard position on the question of what the Negro should do to improve his position in American society argued that racial prejudice was a product of the Negro's condition and not his color. The prejudice of white Americans, these black people believed, would disappear when Negroes improved themselves.[1]

Events after the Civil War suggest that this belief in self-improvement was naive. To be sure, some southern blacks did acquire property, educated their children, and even became respected members of their communities; the vast majority of southern blacks did not, and neither self-improvement nor Methodist discipline changed their lot. Indeed, the emphasis that the A.M.E. Church's hierarchy, laity, and other elite blacks placed on self-improvement, hindsight suggests, was misplaced. The Negro's degraded position in nineteenth-century America was a product of both his color and condition. The interaction of color and condition made black people pariahs. Efforts at ameliorating this situation exacerbated racial conditions as much as it alleviated them. I have tried to illuminate the paradoxical position black people found themselves in during the Civil War and Reconstruction.

1. Cooper, "Elevating the Race: The Social Thought of Black Leaders, 1827–1850"; Sweet, *Black Images of America, 1784–1870*, pp. 108–11.

Bibliography

PRIMARY SOURCES

A.M.E. Materials

The African Methodist Pocket Hymn Book: Selected from Different Authors. Philadelphia: J. H. Cunningham Printer, 1818.

Allen, Richard. *Confessions of John Joyce, alias Davis, who was Executed on Monday the 14th of March, 1808, For the Murder of Mrs. Sarah Cross, with an Address to the Public and People of Colour, Together with the substance of the Trial, and the Address of Chief Justice Tilgham, on His Condemnation.* Philadephia: Printed at No. 12 Walnut Street, 1808. This pamphlet also contains *The Confession of Peter Matthias, Alias Matthews.*

————. *The Life Experience and Gospel Labors of The Rt. Rev. Richard Allen, to which is annexed the Rise and Progress of the African Methodist Episcopal Church in the United States of America.* Also included in this edition is a pamphlet which Allen coauthored with his friend Absalom Jones, *A Narrative of the Proceedings of the Black People during the late awful calamity in Philadelphia in the Year 1793; and Refutation of Some Censures Thrown Upon Them in Some Publications.* Nashville: A.M.E. Sunday School Union, n.d.

Allen, Richard, and Absalom Jones. "Some Letters of Dorothy Ripley," *Journal of Negro History,* I (October, 1916), 436–43.

Allen, Richard, and Jacob Tapisco. *The Doctrines and Disciplines of the African Methodist Episcopal Church.* Philadelphia: n.p., 1819.

Arnett, Benjamin W. *The Budget.* Xenia: Torchlight Printing Co., 1881.

Articles of Association of the African Methodist Episcopal Church of the City of Philadelphia in the Commonwealth of Pennsylvania. Edited by Maxwell Whitman. Originally published 1799. Philadelphia: RHistoric Publications, 1969.

Campbell, Jabez P. *The Doctrine and Discipline of the African Methodist Episcopal Church.* Philadelphia: W. S. Young Co., 1856.

————. "Our Episcopacy," *A.M.E. Review,* VI (July, 1889), 2–3.

Early, Sarah J. *Life and Labors of Rev. Jordan W. Early.* Edited by George A. Singleton. Nashville: A.M.E. Sunday School Union, 1894.

Gaines, Wesley J. *African Methodism in the South or Twenty-five Years of Free-dom*. Atlanta: Franklin Publishing House, 1890.

Handy, James A. *Scraps of African Methodist Episcopal History*. Philadelphia: A.M.E. Book Concern, n.p., n.d.

Jenifer, J. T. "What Has African Methodism to Say As to Its Past? What Has It To Offer the Present? What Does It Promise the Future?" *A.M.E. Review*, III (July, 1884), 251–56.

Payne, Daniel Alexander. "Address to the National Convention of Colored Cit-izens of The United States, at Washington Assembled," printed in *Proceedings of the National Convention of the Colored Men of America, Held in Wash-ington, D.C. on January 13, 14, 15, and 16, 1869*. Washington, D.C.: Great Republican Book and Newspaper Printing Establishment, 1869.

————. *The African Methodist Episcopal Church in Its Relation to the Freed-men*. Xenia: Torchlight Company, 1868.

————. *History of the African Methodist Episcopal Church*. Originally published 1891. New York: Arno Press and New York *Times*, 1969.

————. *The Moral Significance of the 15th Amendment*. Xenia: Printed by the Xenia Gazette Co., 1870.

————. *Recollections of Seventy Years*. Originally published 1888. New York: Arno Press and New York *Times*, 1969.

————, ed. *The Semi-Centenary and the Retrospection of the A.M.E. Church in the U.S.A., 1820–1860*. Baltimore: Sherwood & Co., 1866.

————. *Welcome to the Ransomed, or Duties of the Colored Inhabitants of the District of Columbia*. Baltimore: Bull and Tuttle, 1862.

Payne, Daniel Alexander, and J. M. Brown, eds. *Repository of Religion and Liter-ature and of Science and Art*, Vols. I–IV. Indianapolis & Philadelphia: n.p., 1858–62.

Smith, Charles Spencer. *A History of the African Methodist Episcopal Church*. Philadelphia: A.M.E. Book Concern, 1922.

Steward, Theophilus G. *Fifty Years in the Gospel Ministry*. Philadelphia: A.M.E. Book Concern, 1921.

Tanner, C. M. *Reprint of the First Edition of the Discipline of the A.M.E. Church, with a Historical Preface and Notes*. Atlanta: n.p., 1917.

Tanner, B. T. *An Apology for African Methodism*. Baltimore: Methodist Episco-pal Book Concern, 1883.

————. *An Outline of Our History and Government for African Methodist Churchmen*. Philadelphia: A.M.E. Book Concern, 1884.

Wayman, Alexander W. *Cyclopedia of African Methodism*. Baltimore: Methodist Episcopal Book Depository, 1882.

————. *Manual or Guide Book for the Administration of the Discipline of the A.M.E. Church*. Baltimore: Hoffman & Co., 187?.

————. *My Recollections of African Methodist Episcopal Ministers or Forty Years' Experience in the African Methodist Episcopal Church*. Philadelphia: A.M.E. Book Rooms, 1881.

A.M.E. Conference Records

Journal of the Fifteenth Quadrennial Session of the General Conference of the A.M.E. Church, Nashville, Tennessee, May 6, 1872, n.p., n.d.

Journal of the Sixteenth Session and the Fifteenth Quadrennial Session of the General Conference of the A.M.E. Church, Atlanta, Georgia from May 1 to 18, 1876, n.p, n.d.

Minutes of the Thirty-Second Session of the Ohio Annual Conference of the A.M.E. Church, Held in Zanesville City, Ohio, from April 15 to 23, 1862. Zanesville: The *Daily Courier* Office, 1862.

Minutes of the Pittsburgh Annual Conference of the A.M.E. Church, Held at Brownsville, Pennsylvania, April 15 to 20, 1871. Pittsburgh: W. S. Haven Co., 1871.

Minutes of the Eighth Annual Session of the Virginia Conference of the A.M.E. Church, Assembled in the Town of Danville, Virginia, April 15, 1874. Richmond: Ferguson & Rady, Printers, 1874.

Proceedings of the Eighth General Conference of the A.M.E. Church, Held in the City of Philadelphia, May 1st, 1848. Pittsburgh: Berry F. Patterson Printer, 1848.

Primary Sources General

Allen, William Francis, *et al. Slave Songs of the United States*. Originally published 1867. New York: Peter Smith, 1951.

Benson, Adolph B., ed. *America of the Fifties: Letters of Frederika Bremer*. Originally published 1883. New York: Oxford University Press, 1924.

Blassingame, John W., ed. *Slave Testimony*. Baton Rouge: Louisiana State University Press, 1977.

Borome, Joseph A., ed. "The Autobiography of Hiram Rhodes Revels Together with some Letters by and about Him," *Midwest Journal*, V (1952–53), 79–92.

Butterfield, Lyman, ed. *Letters of Benjamin R. Rush*. 2 vols. Princeton: Princeton University Press, 1951.

Constitution of the American Society of Free Persons of Colour: For Improving Their Condition in the United States; For Purchasing Lands; And for the Establishment of the Convention with Their Address to the Free Persons of Colour in the United States. Edited by Maxwell Whitman. Originally published 1831. Philadelphia: RHistoric Publications, 1969.

The Doctrine and Discipline of the Methodist Episcopal Church. 20th ed. New York: N. Bangs and T. Mason Publishers, 1820.

Fenner, Thomas P. *Cabin and Plantation Songs*. New York: G. P. Putnam's Sons, 1874.

Foner, Philip S., ed. *The Life and Writings of Frederick Douglass: The Civil War*. 4 Vols. New York: International Publishers, 1952.

Garrison, William Lloyd. *Thoughts on African Colonization*. Originally published 1832; New York: Arno Press and New York *Times*, 1968.

Killian, Charles, ed. *Sermons and Addresses, 1853–1891*. New York: Arno Press and New York *Times*, 1972.

Lee, Jarena. *The Life and Religious Experiences of Jarena Lee, Coloured Lady, Giving an Account of Her Call to Preach the Gospel*. Philadelphia: n.p., 1836.

Lynch, James. *The Mission of the United States Republic: An Oration, July 4, 1865*. Augusta, Ga.: Augusta, *Chronicle & Sentinel* Office, 1865.

Osofsky, Gilbert, ed. *Puttin' On Ole Massa*. Originally published 1847. New York: Harper and Row, 1969.

Pearson, Elizabeth Ware, ed. *Letters from Port Royal, 1862–1868.* Originally published 1906. New York: Arno Press and New York *Times,* 1969.

Philips, C. H. *The History of the C.M.E. Church in America.* Jackson: The C.M.E. Church, 1898.

Redkey, Edwin S., ed. *Respect Black: The Writings and Speeches of Henry McNeal Turner, 1863–1906.* New York: Arno Press and New York *Times,* 1971.

Rush, Christopher. *Rise and Progress of the African Methodist Episcopal Church.* New York: Christopher Rush, 1843.

Stearns, Charles. *The Black Man of the South, and the Rebels; or the Characteristics of the Former, and the Recent Outrages of the Latter.* Originally published 1872. New York: Negro University Press, 1969.

Simmons, William J. *Men of Mark.* Originally published 1887. New York: Arno Press and New York *Times,* 1968.

Southey, Robert. *The Life of Wesley and the Rise and Progress of Methodism.* Edited by Rev. J. Atkinson. New York: Frederick Warne Co., 1889.

Steward, Austin. *Twenty-Two Years a Slave and Forty Years a Freeman.* Edited by Jane H. and William H. Pease. Originally published 1857. Reading: Addison Wesley Publishing Co., 1969.

Stuckey, Sterling, ed. *The Ideological Origins of Black Nationalism, 1827–1841.* Reprinted edition. Boston: Beacon Press, 1972.

Webb, Frank J. *The Garies and Their Friends.* Originally published 1857. New York: Arno Press and New York *Times,* 1969.

Yetman, Norman R., ed. *Life Under the Peculiar Institution.* New York: Holt, Rinehart & Winston, Inc., 1970.

Government Documents

Biographical Directory of the American Congress, 1774–1971. Washington: Government Printing Office, 1971.

Candler, Allan D. *The Confederate Records of the State of Georgia.* 6 vols. Atlanta: n.p., 1911.

The Condition of Affairs in the Late Insurrectionary States. 13 vols. Washington: n.p., 1872.

Proceedings of the Constitutional Convention of South Carolina. Originally published 1868. New York: Arno Press and New York *Times,* 1968.

Manuscript Sources

American Missionary Association Papers. Amistad Research Center, Dillard University, New Orleans.

Edward Cary Gardiner Collection. Box 33, Pennsylvania Historical Society, Philadephia.

Sumner, Charles. Correspondence, 1869–1872. Houghton Library, Harvard University, Cambridge.

Newspapers and Journals

The major source for this study was the *Christian Recorder,* especially for the years 1861–1877.

American Union, April 2, 15, 16, 1869; August 27, 1869.
Atlanta Constitution, October 10, 1868; November 28, 1868.
Charleston *Daily Courier*, May 19, 1865.
Colored Tribune, April 15, 1876.
Freedoms Journal, November 2, 1827.
Loyal Georgian, July 6, 1867.
Nation, October 19, 1865, p. 491; May 30, 1867, pp. 432–33.
New Orleans *Tribune*, July 21, 1864; June 9, 1865.
New York *Times*, July 3, 1874.
Savannah *Colored American*, January 13, 1866.
Semi-Weekly *Louisianian*, May 25, 1871.

SECONDARY SOURCES

Books

Adams, Revels. *Cyclopedia of African Methodism in Mississippi*. Natchez: n.p., 1902.
Ahlstrom, Sidney E. *A Religious History of the American People*. New Haven: Yale University Press, 1972.
Barclay, Wade Crawford. *Early American Methodism, 1769–1844*. 2 vols. New York: The Board of Missions and Church Extension of the Methodist Church, 1950.
Benson, Lee. *The Concept of Jacksonian Democracy*. Princeton: Princeton University Press, 1961.
Berlin, Ira. *Slaves Without Masters*. New York: Pantheon Books, 1974.
Berry, Lewellyn Longfellow. *A Century of Missions of the A.M.E. Church*. New York: Guttenberg Printing Co., 1942.
Blassingame, John W. *The Slave Community*. New York: Oxford University Press, 1972.
Brock, W. R. *An American Crisis*. New York: St. Martin's Press, 1963.
Brumm, Ursula. *American Thought and Religious Typology*. Translated by John Hoaglund. New Brunswick: Rutgers University Press, 1970.
Bucke, Emory Stevens, ed. *The History of American Methodism*. 3 vols. New York: Abingdon Press, 1964.
Butt, Israel La Fayette. *History of African Methodism in Virginia*. Norfolk: Hampton Institute Press, 1908.
Chambers, William Nisbet, and Walter Dean Burnham, eds. *The American Party Systems*. 2nd ed. rev. New York: Oxford University Press, 1975.
Clarke, John Henrik, ed. *Ten Black Writers Respond*. Boston: Beacon Press, 1968.
Coan, Josephus R. *Daniel Alexander Payne, Christian Educator*. Philadephia: A.M.E. Book Concern, 1935.
Cornish, Dudley Taylor. *The Sable Arm*. New York: W. W. Norton, 1966.
Coulter, E. Merton. *Negro Legislators in Georgia During the Reconstruction Period*. Athens: Georgia Historical Quarterly, 1968.
Cox, Lawanda and John. *Politics, Principle, and Prejudice, 1865–1866*. New York: Free Press, 1963.

Crum, Mason. *The Negro in the Methodist Church*. New York: Board of Missions and Church Extension of the Methodist Church, 1951.

Du Bois, W. E. B. *Black Reconstruction*. New York: Russell & Russell, 1935.

Duverger, Maurice. *Political Parties*. New York: John Wiley & Sons, 1963.

Farish, Hunter Dickinson. *The Circuit Rider Dismounts: A Social History of Southern Methodism, 1865–1900*. Richmond: Dietz Press, 1938.

Franklin, John Hope. *The Emancipation Proclamation*. New York: Doubleday, 1963.

———. *Reconstruction After the Civil War*. Chicago: University of Chicago Press, 1966

Fredrickson, George M. *The Black Image in the White Mind: The Debate on Afro-American Character and Destiny, 1817–1914*. New York: Harper and Row, 1971.

Foner, Eric. *Free Soil, Free Labor, Free Men*. New York: Oxford University Press, 1970.

Genovese, Eugene D. *Roll, Jordan, Roll*. New York: Pantheon Books, 1974.

George, Carol. *Segregated Sabbaths*. New York: Oxford University Press, 1973.

Gutman, Herbert G. *The Black Family in Slavery and Freedom, 1750–1925*. New York: Pantheon Books, 1976.

Hareven, Tamara K., ed. *Anonymous Americans: Explorations in Nineteenth Century Social History*. Englewood Cliffs: Prentice Hall, 1971.

Huggins, Nathan Irvin. *Slave and Citizen: The Life of Frederick Douglass*. Boston: Little, Brown & Co., 1980.

Jordon, Winthrop D. *White Over Black: American Attitudes Towards the Negro, 1550–1812*. Chapel Hill: University of North Carolina Press, 1968.

Kolchin, Peter. *First Freedom*. Westport: Greenwood Press, 1972.

Lampton, Edward W. *Digest of Rulings and Decisions of the Bishops of the A.M.E. Church from 1847 to 1907*. Washington: Record Publishing Co., 1907.

Levine, Lawrence W. *Black Culture and Black Consciousness*. New York: Oxford University Press, 1977.

Litwack, Leon F. *Been in the Storm So Long*. New York: Alfred A. Knopf, 1979.

———. *North of Slavery*. Chicago: University of Chicago Press, 1961.

McKitrick, Eric. *Andrew Johnson and Reconstruction*. Chicago: University of Chicago Press, 1960.

McPherson, James M. *The Struggle for Equality*. Princeton: Princeton University Press, 1964.

Mathews, Donald G. *Religion in the Old South*. Chicago, University of Chicago Press, 1977.

———. *Slavery and Methodism*. Princeton: Princeton University Press, 1965.

Mathews, Marcia M. *Richard Allen*. Baltimore: Helcion, 1963.

Miller, Floyd J. *The Search for a Black Nationality*. Urbana: University of Illinois Press, 1977.

Mixon, W. H. *History of the African Methodist Episcopal Church in Alabama*. Nashville: A.M.E. Church Sunday School Union, 1902.

Morrow, Ralph E. *Northern Methodism and Reconstruction*. East Lansing: Michigan State University Press, 1956.

Nathans, Elizabeth Studley. *Losing the Peace*. Baton Rouge: Louisiana State University Press, 1968.

Pease, Jane H. and William H. *They Who Would Be Free*. New York: Atheneum, 1974.

Phillips, Ulrich B. *American Negro Slavery*. Originally published 1918. Baton Rouge: Louisiana State University Press, 1966.

Powell, Lawrence N. *New Masters*. New Haven: Yale University Press, 1980.

Quarles, Benjamin. *Lincoln and the Negro*. New York: Oxford University Press, 1962.

Raboteau, Albert J. *Slave Religion: The Invisible Institution in the Antebellum South*. New York: Oxford University Press, 1978.

Randall, James G., and David Donald. *The Civil War and Reconstruction*. Boston: D. C. Heath & Co., 1961.

Rawick, George P. *The American Slave: From Sundown to Sunup*. Westport: Greenwood Press, 1972.

Richardson, Harry V. *Dark Salvation*. Garden City: Anchor Press/Doubleday, 1976.

Richardson, Joe M. *The Negro in the Reconstruction of Florida, 1865–1877*. Tallahassee: Florida State University Press, 1965.

Richards, Leonard L. *Gentlemen of Property and Standing*. New York: Oxford University Press, 1970.

Rosenberg, Bruce A. *The Art of the American Folk Preacher*. New York: Oxford University Press, 1970.

Rothman, David J. *The Discovery of the Asylum*. Boston: Little, Brown & Co., 1971.

Sernett, Milton C. *Black Religion and American Evangelicalism, 1787–1865*. Metuchen, N.J.: Scarecrow and American Theological Library Association, 1975.

Shaw, J. F. *The Negro in the History of Methodism*. Nashville: Parthenon Press, 1954.

Shofner, Jerrell H. *Nor Is It Over Yet: Florida in the Era of Reconstruction, 1863–1877*. Gainesville: University Press of Florida, 1974.

Shugg, Roger W. *Origins of the Class Struggle in Louisiana*. Baton Rouge: Louisiana State University Press, 1939.

Simkins, Francis Butler, and Robert Hilliard Woody. *South Carolina During Reconstruction*. Chapel Hill: University of North Carolina Press, 1932.

Singleton, George A. *The Romance of African Methodism*. New York: Exposition Press, 1952.

Smith, Charles Spencer. *The Life of Daniel Alexander Payne*. Nashville: A.M.E. Publishing House and Church Sunday School Union, 1894.

Smith, J. H. *Vital Facts Concerning the A.M.E. Church*. Published by the Author, 1939.

Stewart, James Brewer. *Holy Warriors*. New York: Hill and Wang, 1976.

Sweet, Leonard I. *Black Images of America, 1784–1870*. New York: W. W. Norton, 1976.

Sweet, William W. *The Methodist Episcopal Church and the Civil War*. Cincinnati: Methodist Book Concern, 1912.

Taylor, E. R. *Methodism and Politics, 1791–1815*. Cambridge: Cambridge University Press, 1935.

Thompson, E. P. *The Making of the English Working Class*. New York: Vintage Books, 1963.

Thurman, Howard. *Jesus and the Disinherited*. New York: Abingdon-Cokesbury Press, 1949.

Toll, William. *The Resurgence of Race.* Philadelphia: Temple University Press, 1979.

Tuveson, Ernest Lee. *Redeemer Nation: The Idea of America's Millenial Role*. Chicago: University of Chicago Press, 1968.

Tyler, Alice Felt. *Freedom's Ferment*. Originally published 1944. New York: Harper Torchbook, 1962.

Wagandt, Charles L. *The Mighty Revolution: Negro Emancipation in Maryland, 1862–1864*. Baltimore: Johns Hopkins University Press, 1964.

Walls, William J. *The African Methodist Episcopal Zion Church*. Charlotte: A.M.E. Zion Publishing House, 1974.

Walters, Ronald G. *American Reformers, 1815–1860*. New York: Hill and Wang, 1978.

Warren, Robert Penn. *The Legacy of the Civil War*. New York: Random House, 1961.

Washington, Joseph R. *Black Religion: The Negro and Christianity in the United States*. Boston: Beacon Press, 1966.

Wearmouth, Robert F. *Methodism and the Working-Class Movements of England, 1800–1850*. London: Epworth Press, 1937.

Welter, Rush. *The Mind of America, 1820–1860*. New York: Columbia University Press, 1975.

Wesley, Charles H. *Richard Allen: Apostle of Freedom*. Washington, D.C.: Associated Publishers, 1935.

Wharton, Vernon Lane. *The Negro in Mississippi, 1865–1890*. Originally published 1947. New York: Harper Torchbook, 1965.

Williamson, Joel. *After Slavery*. Chapel Hill: University of North Carolina Press, 1965.

Wilmore, Gayraud S. *Black Religion and Black Radicalism*. New York: Anchor Press/Doubleday, 1973.

Wright, Richard R., Jr. *The Bishops of the A.M.E. Church*. Nashville: A.M.E. Sunday School Union, 1963.

———, ed. *The Centennial Encyclopedia of the A.M.E. Church*. Philadelphia: Book Concern of the A.M.E. Church, 1916.

———, ed. *Encyclopedia of African Methodism*. Philadelphia: Book Concern of the A.M.E. Church, 1947.

Wolf, William J. *The Religion of Abraham Lincoln*. New York: Seabury Press, 1963.

Wood, Forest G. *The Black Scare*. Berkeley and Los Angeles: University of California Press, 1968.

Woodson, Carter G. *History of the Negro Church*. Washington, D.C.: Associated Publishers, 1921.

Articles

Bacote, Charles A. "William Finch, Negro Councilman, and Political Activities in Atlanta During Early Reconstruction," *Journal of Negro History*, XL (1955), 344–52.

Batten, Minton J. "Henry M. Turner, Negro Bishop Extraordinary," *Church History*, VII (1938), 231–46.
Blassingame, John W. "Selection of Officers and Non-Commissioned Officers of Negro Troops in the Union Army, 1863–1865," *Negro History Bulletin*, XXX (1967), 8–11.
————. "The Union Army As an Educational Institution for Negroes, 1862–1865," *Journal of Negro Education*, XXXIV (1965), 152–59.
Brown, Ira. "Watchers for the Second Coming: The Millenarian Tradition in America," *Mississippi Valley Historical Review*, XXXIX (1952–53), 441–58.
Cooper, Frederick. "Elevating the Race: The Social Thought of Black Leaders, 1827–1850," *American Quarterly*, XXIV (December, 1972), 604–26.
Corson, Fred Pierce. "St. George's Church," in *Historic Philadelphia*. Philadelphia: American Philosophical Society Transactions, 1953.
Dodd, Dorothy. "Bishop Pearce and the Reconstruction of Leon County," *Apalachee: Publication of the Tallahassee Historical Society* (1946), 5–12.
Gottlieb, Manuel. "The Land Question in Georgia During Reconstruction," *Science and Society*, III (1939), 357–59.
Hall, Robert L. "The Gospel According to Radicalism: African Methodism Comes to Tallahassee After the Civil War," *Apalachee: Publication of the Tallahassee Historical Society*, VIII (1971–79), 69–81.
Harding, Vincent. "Religion and Resistance Among Antebellum Negroes, 1800–1860," in August Meier and Elliott Rudwick, eds., *The Making of Black America*. New York: Atheneum, 1969.
Harris, William C. "James Lynch: Black Leader in Southern Reconstruction," *Historian*, XXXIV (1971), 40–61.
Hartzell, Joseph C. "Methodism and the Negro in the United States," *Journal of Negro History*, VIII (July, 1923), 301–15.
Hershberg, Theodore. "Free Blacks in Antebellum Philadelphia: A Study of Ex-Slaves, Freeborn, and Socio Economic Decline," *Journal of Social History*, V (Winter, 1971), 183–209.
Jernegan, Marcus W. "Slavery and Conversion in the Colonies," *American Historical Review*, XXI (1916), 504–27.
Levine, Lawrence W. "Slave Songs and Slave Consciousness: An Exploration in Neglected Sources," in Tamara K. Hareven, ed., *Anonymous Americans: Exploration in Nineteenth Century Social History*. Englewood Cliffs: Prentice-Hall, 1971.
Litwack, Leon. "Free at Last," in Tamara K. Hareven (ed.), *Anonymous Americans: Exploration in Nineteenth Century Social History*. Englewood Cliffs: Prentice-Hall, 1971.
Meier, August. "Negroes in the First and Second Reconstruction," *Civil War History*, XIII (June, 1967), 114–31.
Miller, Floyd J. "The Father of Black Nationalism: Another Contender," *Civil War History*, XVII (1971), 310–20.
Niebuhr, H. Richard. "The Protestant Movement and Democracy in the United States," in James W. Smith and A. Leland Jamison, eds., *The Shaping of American Religion*. Princeton: Princeton University Press, 1961.
Redkey, Edwin. "Bishop Turner's African Dream," *Journal of American History*, LIV (1967), 271–90.

Smith, Timothy. "Slavery and Theology: The Emergence of Black Christian Consciousness in Nineteenth Century America," *Church History*, XLI (1972), 497–512.

Sweet, William W. "The Methodist Episcopal Church and Reconstruction," *Journal of the Illinois State Historical Society*, VII (1914), 147–65.

———. "Methodist Church Influence in Southern Politics," *Mississippi Valley Historical Review*, I (1915), 547–60.

———. "Negro Churches in the South: A Phase of Reconstruction," *Methodist Review*, CIV (1921), 405–18.

Wesley, C. H. "Absalom Jones," in Edwin R. A. Seligman, ed., *Encyclopedia of the Social Sciences*, Vol. VIII. New York: Macmillan, 1932.

Unpublished Material

Ashmore, Nancy Vance. "The Development of the African Methodist Episcopal Church in South Carolina, 1865–1965." M.A. thesis, University of South Carolina, 1969.

Christler, Ethel Maude. "Participation of Negroes in the Government of Georgia, 1867–1870." M.A. thesis, Atlanta University, 1932.

De Boer, Clara. "The Role of Afro-Americans in the Origins and Work of the American Missionary Association." Ph.D. dissertation, Rutgers University, 1973.

Holt, Thomas. "The Emergence of Negro Political Leadership in South Carolina During Reconstruction." Ph.D. dissertation, Yale University, 1973.

Perry, Grace Naomi. "The Educational Work of the A.M.E. Church Prior to 1900." M.A. thesis, Howard University, 1948.

Raboteau, Albert. "The Invisible Institution: The Origins and Conditions of Black Religion Before Emancipation." Ph.D. dissertation, Yale University, 1975.

Washington, James Melvin. "The Origins and Emergence of Black Baptist Separatism, 1863–1897." Ph.D. dissertation, Yale University, 1979.

Winsell, Keith. "*Evolution of Religion Among Negroes in Antebellum America?*" Seminar paper, University of California, Los Angeles, 1967.

Index

DATE DUE

JUN 20 '89			
MAY 23 1995			

HIGHSMITH   #LO-45220